Welcome to A Year with **Yours** 2016 – our annual miscellany packed full of features to keep you entertained and inspired the whole year through.

You can soak up the nostalgia of wonderful reader memories and evocative old photos, or enjoy a look back at our favourite films of yesteryear.

We've got plenty of practical advice, too, with tips to help you stay healthy and expert advice to keep you looking younger. If it's inspiration you're looking for you won't be disappointed. There's a new recipe to try for every week of the year, seasonal craft projects to have a go at and lots of ideas to motivate you to get outside in the garden. There are laughs, quizzes, poems, puzzles and stories too; there really is something for everyone!

This book is truly individual – created with the help of **Yours** readers. It's their stories that make this yearbook special and my sincere thanks goes to all who contributed, including those whose letters we didn't have room to publish.

Happy reading – and all the best for 2016

Sharon

Sharon Reid
Editor, **Yours** Magazine

Published by Pedigree in association with **Yours**
Pedigree Books Limited, Beech House, Walnut Gardens, Exeter, Devon EX4 4DH

Yours – the read of your life every fortnight! Look out for it in your local newsagent.
Yours, Bauer London Lifestyle, Media House, Peterborough Business Park, Peterborough PE2 6EA.
Tel: 01733 468000

Compiled and edited by Sharon Reid
Designed by David Reid
Sub-edited by Christine Curtis
Additional writing by Marion Clarke, Lizzy Denning, Lynne Ewart, Alex Frisby, Valery McConnell, Rebecca Speechley, Claire Williams and Katharine Wootton
Story illustrations by Kate Burgess

◆ All telephone numbers, website details and dates correct at time of going to press

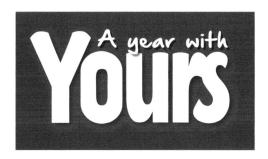

Name _Klendoreen_

Address

Postcode

Home phone

Mobile phone

Email

In case of emergency, contact:

Name

Telephone

Useful contacts

Bank	
Building society	
Chemist/pharmacy	
Chiropodist	
Council	
Credit card emergency	
Dentist	
Doctor	
Electrician	
Garage	
Hairdresser	
Hospital	
Local police	
Milkman	
Optician	
Plumber	
Solicitor	
Taxi	
Vet	

Renewal reminders

	Renewal date	Policy number	Telephone
Car insurance			
Car tax			
MOT			
Home insurance			
TV licence			
Pet insurance			
Yours subscription			

THE YEAR AHEAD

Make 2016 your healthiest year yet

Challenge yourself to be a healthier new you – one step at a time

If you're after a fresh start this New Year, don't make any resolutions… they're rarely successful. In fact, just eight per cent of people will achieve their goals. Most of us set unrealistic targets – aiming to shed stones, overhaul our diets or give up alcohol entirely. When it comes to swapping your unhealthy habits for healthy ones it's best to change one thing at a time. If you want to eat better, exercise more and quit smoking, trying to do them all at once will make you miserable and probably lead to failure. But if you focus on one goal and take small steps to achieve it you're more likely to succeed. To help you along we've set you some simple health goals to work towards each month – and by the end of the year you should feel healthier, happier and more energetic. Get started today.

January

"I will eat one more portion of fruit and veg a day"

We all know that we should be eating five portions of fruit and vegetables a day – but sometimes reaching that target can be difficult. Eating enough fruit and veg could reduce your risk of health problems such as heart disease and cancer, and according to researchers it could help you live longer in good health. The good news is that any extra fruit or veg helps. Scientists have found that for every piece of fruit of veg you eat there is a five per cent reduction in the risk of dying from all causes. That's good news if you ask us. Try adding an extra portion to you diet every day.

One portion is equal to 80g (3oz) which is one apple, pear, orange or banana, a dessert bowl of salad or three heaped tablespoons of peas, beans or pulses. Snack on an apple, have salad with your pasta or toss a tablespoon of raisins into your cereal.

February

"I will take a daily walk"

Regular exercise helps to keep your heart and lungs healthy, strengthens your bones, helps you maintain a healthy weight and stay mobile. A daily walk could really benefit your health. Research has shown that taking just 2000 extra steps a day (that's about one mile) could reduce you risk of heart disease by eight per cent. For extra benefits and motivation take a brisk walk with a friend or join a walking group, another study found that walking in a group helps to lower your blood pressure, body fat, body mass index, resting heart rate and total cholesterol – making you generally much healthier. This month add a daily 20-minute walk to your diary and you'll soon see the benefits. If 20 minutes seems too much to fit in – just put your coat on and walk around the block – getting started is often the biggest battle.

Top tip

Each month plan how you will tackle each challenge – schedule time in your day, add healthy ingredients to your shopping list and get the support of your friends – the more organised you are the less chance you'll have for slip ups.

March

"I will drink one less glass of alcohol a day"

A glass of wine a day could reduce your risk of heart disease in later life and according to some studies even boost your brain power. But many of us drink more than that putting ourselves at risk of high blood pressure, stroke, liver disease and cancer. Cutting down to just one glass of wine a day (a 175ml/6floz glass is around two units) is best for your health. If you regularly drink more than this then try to gradually cut down by a glass a day. Men should have no more than four units of alcohol a day, which is equivalent to one pint of beer.

Don't forget to check the alcohol percentage of what you're drinking – for example a 175ml (6 floz) glass of 11 per cent alcohol volume is 1.9 units, whereas the equivalent amount of a 14 per cent wine is 2.4 units.

April

"I will eat one portion of oily fish a week"

Eating one portion of oily fish a week could halve your risk of developing rheumatoid arthritis according to a Swedish study. Oily fish contain healthy omega-3 fatty acids, which are thought to help reduce inflammation in your body. They're also known to be good for your heart and brain health.

Salmon, sardines, mackerel, trout and whitebait are all good sources of omega-3 fats. Current guidelines suggest that women should have at least two 140g (5oz) portions of fish a week, one of which should be oily fish. Try a trout salad, a salmon and avocado sandwich or a seafood stew. ➡

May

"I will stand on one leg"

How good is your balance? How long you can stand on one leg could be an indication of your wider health. Researchers timed how long people could stand on one leg with their eyes closed and followed up the data with them 10 years later. Those who could stand on one leg for the longest (up to 30 seconds) were more likely to be in good health, while those who struggled to balance had a higher risk of health problems.

Good balance has also been linked to stronger bones, lower risk of falls and a healthy brain. Practise balancing by standing on one leg for as long as you can each day. Start by holding on to a chair and as you build up strength let go to improve your balance. Make sure you pay equal attention to each leg.

June

"I will swap white bread for brown"

Swapping to wholegrain carbohydrates such as brown rice, wholewheat pasta and wholemeal bread could help you to lose weight. Refined carbs such as white rice, bread, sugary foods and pasta give you a spike of energy that quickly sends your blood sugar plummeting, leaving you feeling hungry and tired. Wholegrain carbs, on the other hand, take longer to digest, keeping you feeling fuller for longer and taking away the urge to snack.

One study found that dieters on a low GL diet plan, which includes wholegrain carbs, lost on average 2.2 pounds more than people on other diets. Try swapping your usual cereal for porridge, use wholemeal bread to make a sandwich and brown rice, wholewheat pasta or a sweet potato with your evening meal.

Top tip

Write your monthly promises out and stick them on your fridge or somewhere prominent to remind you of your goal.

Top tip

Be prepared for slip-ups... there will be days that you miss your goal, but don't let that stop you. Keep trying to introduce healthy habits into your life and it will soon become second nature.

July

"I will swap a hot drink a day for water"

Coffee and tea contain caffeine, which in small doses can be good for your health. One study found that moderate coffee drinking could help to keep your arteries clear and prevent Atherosclerosis (furring of your arteries which could contribute to heart problems). But drinking more than 400mg of caffeine a day – that's about four cups of coffee or five cups of tea – could cause sleep problems, contribute to anxiety and increase your heart rate.

Caffeine is also a diuretic and could leave you dehydrated, which could make you feel tired and in need of yet another cup of coffee. So this month try swapping one cuppa for a glass of water and see how you feel. Some experts suggest we should aim to drink two litres of water a day to help our health and energy levels – that's about eight glasses.

August

"I will try yoga"

Practising yoga regularly could make a huge difference to your health. Researchers have found that yoga is as good for your heart as walking or cycling, while another study discovered that it could help to improve your memory and attention span.

Further research suggests that it could help to ease back pain too. The postures help to improve balance, tone you up and stretch tired muscles, while the controlled breathing helps to reduce stress. Your yoga teacher will help you adapt postures for your ability and you can work at your own pace. Try a class once a week for a month.

Check local listings for a class near you, or find a teacher at 01529 306851 (www.bwy.org.uk) ➡

PICS: ALAMY

Top tip

Think about how you want to feel – each month look at your goal and think about how achieving it will make you feel – will you have more energy, a smaller waist, feel less guilty about what you eat? Then focus on that positive feeling to get you through the tricky times.

September

"I will take Vitamin D every day"

As the days get shorter and darker it's hard to keep our Vitamin D levels topped up. Your body makes Vitamin D from sunlight and we don't get enough in the winter months in the UK, so it's a good idea to take a Vitamin D supplement every day.

Studies have shown that Vitamin D could help to support your immune system and bone health. And further research suggests that people with low levels of Vitamin D in their bodies are more susceptible to Seasonal Affective Disorder (SAD). SAD can lead to low mood, weight gain and fatigue. Oily fish are a good source of Vitamin D, but it's best to take a supplement so make a promise to take one every day this month or even better throughout the winter.

October

"I will spend time with friends every week"

It's tempting to hunker down indoors as the weather gets colder and you may feel less sociable – but it's important to make the effort to see your friends and family.

Loneliness can lead to low mood and comfort eating, causing us to eat unhealthy foods and gain weight, according to US scientists. On the other hand, having a good giggle and a catch up with friends causes your brain to release endorphins, which could help to ease pain and lift your mood.

Arrange a weekly catch up with a good friend, join an evening class or take up a new hobby to get you out of the house. If it's not easy for you to get out and about, telephone a friend at least once a week for a chat.

And if you're feeling lonely call Silverline 24 hours a day for advice or a chat 0800 4 70 80 90.

November

"I will get a good night's sleep"

It's normal for us to sleep a bit less as we get older, but you should still wake up feeling refreshed. Getting a decent night's sleep is important for your health, too, because lack of sleep could increase your risk of high blood pressure and memory problems.

Try to keep to a similar sleep routine, getting up and going to bed at the same times each day. Signal to your body that it's time to sleep by doing something relaxing just before you turn in – it could be reading a book, some gentle stretches or having a warm bath.

If you struggle to get enough sleep because you wake up feeling anxious try going to bed earlier. US researchers have found that turning in early could help to reduce the number of negative thoughts you experience. This month try to go to bed a little earlier and set up a sleep routine to help you wake up feeling energised.

December

"I will take 10 minutes of 'me time' a day"

The festive season can be stressful, with presents to buy, grandchildren to calm down, family squabbles to deal with and a big lunch to cook. It can be hard not to become overwhelmed. Feeling stressed can raise your blood pressure, slow your digestion and weaken your immune system. It can even make it harder for you to cope with pain.

Look for a time of day when you can fit in a bit of 'me time'. It only needs to be ten minutes sitting quietly by yourself doing something that you enjoy or just organising your mind and taking a few deep breaths. And try to stick to it – after all looking after yourself is really important.

25 ways to look 10 years younger!

Knock off a decade with these easy expert tips

PICS: ALAMY

Skincare problem solving

When it comes to problem skin, you just need to know what to look for. Skincare expert Sally Penfold picks her must-have ingredients for mature skin...

Keep wrinkles at bay

"Prevention is better than cure, so stop lines becoming any deeper by ensuring you're using a daily sun protection of at least SPF15," says Sally. "My favourite anti-ageing ingredient is pure Vitamin A, sometimes known as retinol, which can reverse UV damage and prompt cell recovery. Your skin will appear plumper and smoother with just one great product."

Clear excess oil

"Going through the menopause can leave your skin more oily, because of an imbalance of testosterone," says Sally. "Combat this by switching to a clay-based cleanser, which will mop up oil and deep clean skin. If the oil has also increased your pore size, use the same cleanser twice a week as a mini facemask, leaving on for 10 minutes, to clean deep into your pores and clear excess oil."

Stay hydrated

"Watch your caffeine intake, turn down the central heating and use a moisturiser rich in hyaluronic acid," says Sally. "This ingredient holds about 1,000 times its own weight in water, providing amazing hydration for thirsty skin.

Banish age spots

"If you have excess pigmentation or 'age spots' look for skin-brightening products with ingredients such as liquorice, Vitamin C and kiwi, and use morning and night to slow down your production of melanin (brown pigment)," says Sally.

Be super smooth

"To instantly smooth dry skin, look no further than a good quality exfoliant," says Sally. "If you have sensitive skin, look for a gentle product with rice bran powder, or otherwise try a lactic acid-based mask, for smoother, more radiant skin."

5 DIY anti-ageing treats

Raid your kitchen for some youth-boosting pampering!

1 For softer, stronger hair, create your own hair mask with raw eggs. Mix two-three (depending on your hair length) in a cup and apply evenly to dry hair. Leave for 20-25 minutes and wash out thoroughly before shampooing and conditioning as normal. Try this once a month and you'll notice the difference.

2 For brighter skin in just 15 minutes, mash together half a banana, one tablespoon of fresh orange juice and one tablespoon of clear honey for a soothing face-mask treat. The Vitamin B in the banana will brighten, while the honey will help moisturise.

3 If you have sensitive or oily skin, oatmeal should be your best friend. Mix two tablespoons of oatmeal with a tablespoon of rosewater and a tablespoon of natural honey for a gentle mask that will draw out excess oil. Relax for ten minutes before washing off.

4 Curled lashes will instantly make your eyes seem wider and brighter. Make your own 'curlers' by heating a teaspoon in warm water, drying it, and holding it gently against your upper lashes to set a curve.

5 Create a youthful sheen on dry or dull skin by mixing a drop of olive oil into your foundation before application. ➡

Beautiful skin, day and night

With so many products on offer, all promising to deliver anti-ageing results, it can be difficult to know what to buy – and when to use it. Marie McKeever, Head of Treatment Development at Clarins has cut through the jargon to create a simple day to night routine

What should we be doing first thing?

"In the morning, after washing or cleansing your face, it's worth adding a serum to your routine, before moisturising with a light, easily absorbed day cream," says Marie. "Serums enhance the skin, making it look fresher, as well as helping it to absorb all the moisture from a day cream and stay hydrated for longer. "Don't forget to protect your hands too – buy a hand cream with an SPF, and keep them topped up throughout the day to prevent age spots."

What are the key ingredients to look for in a day cream?

"The plant extract harungana will replenish and regenerate the skin, while oat sugars and tomato extracts will both firm slackening skin. Vitamin C will brighten a dull complexion and help to balance

MAGIC MAKE-UP TIP:
If you have dry skin, choose rich, illuminating foundations and cream eye shadows. To set your skin with a powder, pick a mineral product which won't go dry and cakey.

MAGIC MAKE-UP TIP:
Fuller eyebrows will bring out your eyes and give your face a more youthful, put-together appearance. Fill them in with a soft brow pencil or taupe/brown coloured eye shadow for a soft, natural finish

age spots, while Vitamin E and omega-3 fatty acids will add oil to moisturise and plump your face. If you're ever in any doubt, it's always worth talking to the experts at beauty counters, as they will know more about ingredients and anti-ageing properties in all of their products. Don't be afraid to take some samples away to try before buying. Once you've invested, keep your moisturiser in the fridge – the cooler temperature will help reduce your pore size and keep excess oil to a minimum."

What can I do to hide the signs of ageing on my neck?

"Never underestimate the power of water. Start your day with a cold shot of water in the shower – it might not feel very nice, but it will shock your skin into tightening and lifting, and it will certainly wake you up! Doing this every morning will boost the firmness of your neck and décolleté."

How should our night routine differ?

"Night time is when the body rests and the skin comes to life! Cleanse carefully with a cream or oil, and lots of gentle facial massaging movements with your fingertips to stimulate circulation and boost radiance. Then use a rich night cream to feed the skin and help repair any damage done throughout the day. Heighten the results by mixing in a few drops of a beauty oil – these are super heroes for moisture-starved skin."

Give your hair a youth boost

Tackle the top mature hair problems for younger-looking tresses every day

MAGIC MAKE-UP TIP: Swap your powder for a cream blush – these leave you with a soft, dewy finish.

Go grey with grace

Grey hair no longer means looking like your granny did, with gorgeous actresses from Helen Mirren to Julie Walters all looking fabulous in silver tones. "Fresh highlights and flattering layers will really update grey hair," says Skyler McDonald, Creative Director at seanhanna, "but it can need a little more TLC, so make sure to use a hair mask regularly. This will really condition and smooth your hair cuticles and make it look thicker and more lustrous."

Fight the frizz!

Nothing is more ageing than dry, brittle hair, but with a little care soft, youthful tresses can be yours once more. "A big mistake many people make is roughly towel-drying their hair, which causes it to become static," says Skyler. "To protect it from damage, gently and slowly squeeze water out of it instead, using your hands and then a towel. After blow drying, add some hair serum for a shiny finish." End your blow dry with a blast of cold air – it will leave your locks looking shiny all day long.

Fine time

Make thinning hair seem thicker with the right products. "Fine hair can get weighed down by shampoo," says Skyler. "Gentle shampoos marked for volume and daily/frequent washing are your best bets. The product should be clear, not thick and creamy. To combat build-up, wash it once a week with a clarifying shampoo, or rinse it with a mixture of one third apple cider vinegar and two thirds water."

What massage techniques can I use in the evening?

"Boost your circulation and bring a glow to your face with some easy facial massage. After applying facial oil or moisturiser, place your hands horizontally from your jawline, fingers facing your nose, and lift them upwards towards your eyes one hand at a time. Vary the speed to increase the rate at which your skin absorbs the product's active ingredients. Then move up to your forehead, stroking from your eyebrows to your hairline."

MAGIC MAKE-UP TIP: Use a primer before foundation to smooth away fine lines, even out your complexion and keep make up in place.

PICS: ALAMY

Your stars for the

All the predictions for 2016 from **Yours** astrologer Lynne Ewart

ARIES

March 21 – April 20

Ruled by action planet Mars, you thrive on challenges, preferably set by yourself. You are someone who needs to lead the way, rather than to be too boxed in by a fixed regime. You love nothing better than to leap into action at short notice to be the hero for another. What you can't bear is to be dependent on others, or to have to sit sweetly awaiting another's instruction. Not for you a dull or boring life and even if that madly impulsive and headstrong quality, which often materialises in youth, is toned down, the flames of passion for life's adventures never quite do. 2016 brings fresh commitment to improving skills, fitness and surroundings.

PEOPLE & PLEASURES

You're often drawn to partners and pals who share your spirit of adventure, but who may be just that bit more 'earthed' or practical than you are, although you do love to be with creative and fun-loving people, too. Aries often seems to encounter people with star quality, perhaps reflecting some of your own hidden talents. Don't be afraid to have a go at the skills you so admire in others. Join that class, explore that interest a little further, and never think the time has passed to tackle a new quest!

MAKE 2016... the year to learn or teach something that truly lights your spirit up.

TAURUS

April 21 – May 21

Steady as an oak tree, you are that wonderfully calming person who everyone comes to when they feel unsettled or out of sorts. Harmony-loving Venus rules your sign, and you really do a lot to keep life purring along smoothly, withstanding the slings and arrows of outrageous fortune, weathering storms like that oak tree, but sometimes feeling the stress and finding it hard to handle, so try not to take on too much! 2016 is a year of opportunity to widen your circle of friends, and could bring several special family celebrations. Baby news could delight many a Taurean!

PEOPLE & PLEASURES

Taurus is a sensual, comfort-loving sign, and you love nothing better than a cuppa and a catch-up with favourite people. Soothing is something you do a lot of, so you'll need some of that back, too, to keep things balanced, and that comes in the form of good food and the company of light-hearted characters who, ideally, make you feel young and carefree! Dancing often appeals, and there's often a flirtatious sparkle in the eye of a Taurean, ruled as you are by the love goddess herself, so joining a dance class could be great for fun and friendship.

MAKE 2016... a year for reconnections and revivals that'll bring you joy.

year ahead

GEMINI
May 22 – June 21

You are such an enigma, being born under the sign of the twins, one shy and one chatty. It often takes until midlife for a Gemini to fully blossom and to start celebrating rather than criticising those restless, ever-curious, never-quite-settled traits which actually keep you thoroughly fascinating to the rest of us! You stay so youthful because you're always busy looking at the next interesting idea and you rarely seem to have time to dwell on the past. Geminis are such fun. Everyone should know at least one. 2016 is about partnerships and happy homemaking.

PEOPLE & PLEASURES
Bold, adventurous people intrigue you, as do artistic types. You're at your happiest when quizzing someone about a person, place or event of interest, although few can keep up with your rapid-fire questions! It's not that you are a gossip, but you seem to know everything that's going on, and lively, sociable characters will always appeal. You also connect with gentle, home-lovers who understand that you may be a butterfly, but you always fly home. An outdoor interest that gives a rush of fresh air, whether it's walking, sailing, riding or skiing is good for your soul.

MAKE 2016... your time to get your home life working just right.

CANCER
June 22 – July 22

Your sensitivity makes you a wonderful friend, parent or lover. It also drives you nuts if you feel hurt or unsure of others. You have a tough outer shell for a reason. Once you let folk close you feel more vulnerable. But with maturity you discard the shell and live a little more hopefully. You are one of life's 'feeders', often found in the kitchen, clucking and caretaking. You see the past as a treasure chest of knowledge and power, but find it hard to let go of feelings. 2016 has an uplifting quality, great for expanding the mind and developing useful skills.

PEOPLE & PLEASURES
In friendship, you are someone who will be there in a crisis, supporting and providing soul food. Personally, you are drawn to careful characters who make you feel secure and safe. Family will always be at the deepest core of your world, though, and if you have none, you'll find friends who feel like family, people you're completely at ease with, when your hair's messy and you're in your cosy clothes. You are very real, and you love to nurture folk, so your place will always feel homely and welcoming, and there'll usually be food on the go! Photography and culinary classes might attract you.

MAKE 2016... the year you believe in a talent that enriches you. ➡

LEO
July 23 – August 23

You are someone who naturally radiates warmth and charisma, even if you're one of those more self-conscious lions or lionesses, people gravitate to you, and your place is often where everyone wants to be. As a host or hostess you are exquisite, aware of what delights, and as a friend as well as in the role of parent you are generous and stubbornly, endearingly loyal. 2016 sees you achieving goals that might involve streamlining, either with resources or in a physical sense. This will be a year of shedding what holds you back, so you may well be making good health choices.

PEOPLE & PLEASURES

Life needs to be lived fully when you are a Leo, and with positive, energetic characters who'll inspire you to be all you can be and then some! You were born to shine, and for that light to warm the hearts of others. Fine looking, well-presented people attract you, but it takes a fine, sharp mind and an independent spirit to hold your attention for any length of time. Leo can be a performer or an artist, but is usually someone who loves great shows, so interests that take you towards the arts and to drama can light you up.

MAKE 2016... the year you accept a life-enhancing challenge!

VIRGO
August 24 – September 22

The essential Virgoan is self-contained – always processing information and soaking in the detail with senses alight. You are modest, careful and reserved, at least until you have fully assessed a person or situation. You are as capable of letting your hair down and dancing on the table as anyone else, but only if the circumstances feel comfortable. Virgos want time to think, unless someone needs help, in which case you're right there. 2016 is a year of liberation, letting go of the old, and of doors opening where you possibly thought there were none. Prepare to be surprised by your own panache.

PEOPLE & PLEASURES

Much as you appreciate the efforts others go to in order to look fabulous, you really love to be with someone who's travelled, learned and had strong life experiences. Yes, you might have a giggle at the gossip, but mostly you'd sooner be impressed by achievements and by people who go the extra mile in life to do their best by themselves and others. Your love of fine detail might tug you towards crafting, and a writers' workshop could intrigue you. Being an earth sign, it does your soul good to be in the outdoors, connecting with Mother Nature, too.

MAKE 2016... the year you decide to do something good for YOU!

LIBRA
September 23 – October 23

As an air sign, you need time to think, to ponder every side of a question, which is why you can sometimes be found sitting on the fence, as your logical mind and your innate desire for easy harmony tugs you to always see all the angles – never just one viewpoint. For that reason you can seem indecisive, but also make a lot of friends who hugely appreciate that breadth of vision. Libra, you are in a highly karmic 'reward' phase, with good things coming your way when least expected. Luck will find you in some rather unusual ways as 2016 unfolds.

PEOPLE & PLEASURES

Relationships matter hugely, and you are a gracious, courteous social creature who appreciates the feeling of being balanced by a partnership. Some Librans are single forever but have a special pal or pet who creates that balance. Gentle, clever minds attract you, and being ruled by Venus, you love art and beauty. Getting involved with something artistic or into a partnered or team activity can appeal. Librans are forever stylish, so you appreciate a well-groomed mate. Nails need to be tidy too! Meeting friends for a chat over your favourite tipple, be it cappuccino or Chardonnay, soothes your soul.

MAKE 2016... the year you listen to your intuitive self.

SCORPIO
October 24 – Nov 22

Ruler planet Pluto brings deeper life experiences to most born under Scorpio. Upheavals and emotional turmoil often follow in your wake, and yet with each bump in the road, your strength, courage and resilience increases, as does your insight and, my goodness, your problem-solving skills are second to none. You are the Phoenix – never forget that! You arrived here on planet Earth already destined for times of rebirthing and for many fresh chapters. Not for you a dull life. 2016 brings significant wheeling and dealing, possibly career negotiations and perhaps a new financial or resource-seeking role within a group.

PEOPLE & PLEASURES

Scorpio appreciates trust and you draw confidence from others, often in the most unlikely settings! You are a wonderful listener, which means a lot. Reiki and reflexology can attract, and you do love a good thriller, quickly guessing whodunnit! You sometimes attract people whose lives are complex and, although you are well equipped to handle challenges, it does you good to be with people who make you giggle. Amateur dramatics can be a marvellous outlet for your fascination with human nature while your secretive 'poker face' is great for playing Bridge!

MAKE 2016... your year to shed something that's been holding you back. ➡

SAGITTARIUS
November 23 – December 21

The classic Sagittarius is a positive thinker; rarely stopping to dwell on a problem, way too busy seeking the solution. Your nature tends to be open and direct, and you value your freedom so much, you need to be able to travel, to be on the move. Independence is always your intention, so you will do whatever it takes to stay fit and mobile! You're just the most fun when you're full of enthusiasm for a new adventure, and you love the thrill of a new goal. 2016 brings a new role or title, and possibly a building project.

PEOPLE & PLEASURES
Cheery, bright and sunny-natured folk light you up and gain your attention very easily, while overly serious or sensitive characters tend to dim your light a little. You can be a wonderfully understanding friend who will give wise advice, but you believe in keeping moving forward so you tend to like folk who, like you, see the future as an adventure waiting to happen and the past as a story where you know the outcome, so it's not as fascinating as galloping forwards. Travel, ideally across beautiful scenery, learning new things and being with knowledgeable people makes you happy.

MAKE 2016... the year you steer your way to a golden ambition.

CAPRICORN
December 22 – January 20

Planet Saturn is associated with Capricorn because he's all about timing, about looking before you leap, being security minded. Not for you is the fast-fix or low-cost merchandise that falls apart within months. You want your resources to go where they'll last longest. Capricorn seems serious when younger, perhaps carrying a great weight of the expectations of others. You are a hard worker but the older you get the lighter your step becomes, and the more your sense of humour sparkles. 2016 is a good year for studying something you wished you'd learned more about, at school.

PEOPLE & PLEASURES
You are a classy dresser as a rule, more elegant than trendy, often deliciously thrifty about recycling. Finding a cashmere coat in a charity shop could delight the typical Capricorn! You can come across as fairly reserved, while quietly getting the measure of another, but when you turn on the full beam of your charismatic charm, few have the defences to resist you! The eyes of a Capricorn are rarely as serious as their demeanour! You are attracted to a steadfast mate who, ideally, can cook and who entertains well. You do love stimulating chat over a nice meal!

MAKE 2016... a year to tap into underused talents that'll widen your horizons.

AQUARIUS
January 21 – February 18

As an air sign, you have a hunger for knowledge and you make connections with a wide, eclectic social circle, needing lots of personal space to circulate. You love a cosy home life but you also crave the rush of fresh air and the stimulation of fresh ideas that comes from being out and about. Ruled by cranky Uranus, you can be opinionated and stubborn, but you can also be won over with clever humour! 2016 holds an eclipse path that could bring some unusual benefits by the autumn, effecting you either physically or financially, perhaps both.

PEOPLE & PLEASURES
Mental pleasures are uppermost whether you are playing chess, doing quizzes or reading. Aquarians usually read a lot, and you also tend to be one of the most technologically savvy characters, or if not, you'll always know someone who'll help you set up the latest tablet, e-reader or computer. To attract your interest a potential friend or partner will have a clever mind combined with an independent, self-contained nature, someone who doesn't need constant reassurance that you care. Aquarians often have an affinity with both the people and the foods of the Orient, so Japanese, Thai, Vietnamese or Chinese restaurants could appeal.

MAKE 2016... a retro year as you revive old hobbies or revisit favourite haunts!

PISCES
February 19 – March 20

You are the intuitive dreamer who loves to drift into a world of imagination, being swept away on a tide of emotion, appreciating nature, listening to music or immersing yourself in a movie. Yet, you are often handed a life path that demands you have your feet on the ground, looking after others, overlooking yourself. In true Cinderella style though, your life will also contain moments of magic where kindnesses are rewarded when least expected. 2016 is your time to reach for the stars, when the support of good people can spur you on to a fabulous achievement. Never say never!

PEOPLE & PLEASURES
Ideally, Pisceans should mix with earthy, steady partners and pals, and you do, often finding lifelong friendships with those characters. But you are like a magnet too for those whose highs and lows in life will take you on quite a rollercoaster ride, so partnerships tend to be quite eventful and even a little crazy at times, but never dull! You enjoy travel, and music and laughter, but friendly as you are, you also need to have peaceful little capsules of time every now and then where you can recharge your batteries in tranquil surroundings, maybe with a good book.

MAKE 2016... your time to shine with pride in your own capabilities.

Pretty kitchen cosies

You will need:

(For one tea cosy and two matching egg cosies)
Pen/pencil
Card
Scissors
Fabric glue
1m (1yd) light blue fleece
15cm (6in) square of
pink felt fabric
50cm (20in) square of
yellow fleece
9 orange buttons 1cm (¹/₂in) in
diameter for the tea cosy and
1 for each egg cosy
Orange embroidery floss
(thread)
Basic sewing kit

Brighten up your morning routine with these pretty and practical floral cosies

To make the tea cosy:

1 Draw a tea cosy template on to card, measure it against your teapot to make sure it will cover completely and cut out. Place on the wrong side of the light blue fleece (on the grain line). Using a permanent marker pen, draw around it four times. Cut out two pieces.

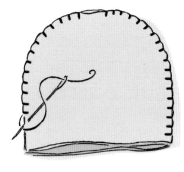

2 Place the pieces together in pairs, with the wrong sides together. Place these pairs together and pin around the sides to hold. Stitching through two layers, work a blanket stitch around the curved outside edge in orange embroidery floss (thread), leaving the straight bottom edge open and a small gap at the top for the felt loop.

3 Blanket stitch the straight bottom edges of the front and back of the cozy, stitching through one layer of fleece at a time.

4 Cut out one 5x2cm (2x¾in) strip of pink felt to make a loop. Place inside the unstitched gap at the centre top of the tea cozy and attach using fabric glue.

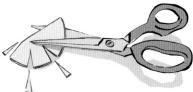

5 Draw a circle 6cm (2¹/₂in) in diameter on card and cut out. Place on the wrong side of the yellow fleece, draw around it nine times, and cut out.

6 Fold each fleece circle in half, wrong sides together. Pin to hold, and make five small wedge-shaped snips evenly around the semicircles to make petals. Open out the circle, then cut a curved shape around the top of each petal.

7 Using the photo as a guide, position the yellow fleece flowers on the tea cosy and attach using fabric glue. Glue an orange button to the center of each flower.

To make the egg cosies:

The egg cosies are made in exactly the same way as the tea cosy, but you will only need to cut out one flower, not 9.

Project taken from Fleece Fantastic by Rachel Henderson, published by CICO Books (£12.99). Photos © Penny Wincer.

Keep-it-cool bags

Bring a zing of summer to any picnic with these oilcloth lunch bags and bottle coolers

You will need:

For the bag:
Oilcloth measuring 28x62cm (11x24½in)
Thermal insulated batting (wadding) measuring 28x62cm (11x24½in)
Rubberised cotton measuring 27x61cm (10½x24 in).
1.3cm (½in) wide bias binding measuring 56cm (22in) in length
2.5cm (1in) wide cotton tape measuring 20 cm (8in) in length

For the bottle cooler:
Oilcloth measuring 17x62cm (6¾x24½in)
Thermal insulated batting (wadding) measuring 17x62cm (6¾x24½in)
Rubberised cotton measuring 16x61cm (6¼x24in)
3cm (1¼in) wide bias binding measuring 34cm (13½in) in length
2.5cm (1in) wide cotton tape measuring 48cm (19in) in length
Pins
Scissors
Sewing machine
Ruler
Pencil

1 To make the bag, place the oilcloth wrong side up on your work surface and place the thermal batting (wadding) on top, aligning all the edges. Fold the oilcloth and batting (wadding) in half, short edge to short edge, and with the right sides facing. Pin and sew down each side with a 1cm (1in) seam allowance. Trim the seam allowance back to approximately 3mm (⅛in) and turn the right way out.

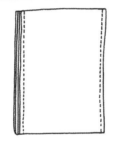

2 Squash the bag flat, so that the two side seams are at the centre and the bottom of the bag extends as two triangles front and back. Using a ruler and a pencil, draw a line across the base of the triangle at the front of the bag and 6cm (2½in) in from the point of the triangle.

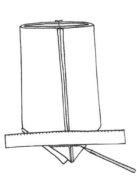

3 Stitch along the line you drew in step 2 and trim to remove the triangle. Repeat on the triangle at the back of the bag. Open the bag out and stand on its base.

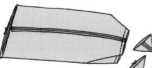

4 Make the bag lining from the rubberized cotton in the same way, but don't turn it the right way out.

5 With wrong sides facing, place the lining inside the outer bag, matching up the side seams.

6 Starting at one of the side seams, fold the bias binding in half over the top edge of the bag and pin in position. It's best to have the bias binding a little deeper on the inside of the bag than it is on the outside. This way, when you sew the binding close to the edge on the front, you will catch all of the binding on the inside. Fold the raw edges under at the ends of the bias binding and overlap them by 1cm (½in) Sew a line of stitching to attach.

7 Cut the cotton tape in two to make one length that measures 26cm (10½in) and one 22cm (8¾in) in length. Fold under 2cm (¾in) at the raw end of the longer length and pin it to the bag, centred on the front and 17cm (6¾in) from the top edge.

8 Sew the tape to the bag, making a square of stitches to secure the folded under end of the tape (see illustration). Reinforce the stitching by sewing two diagonals lines across the square.

9 Repeat Step 8 with the shorter length of tape. Centre the tape on the opposite side of the bag and 4cm (1½in) down from the top edge.

10 Make the bottle cooler in exactly the same way. At Step 7, cut the cotton tape so that one length is 2cm (¾in) longer at one end.

Project taken from A Year in Crafts by Clare Youngs, published by CICO Books (£14.99). Photos © Joanna Henderson.

Rag rug

Transform a couple of old bedcovers into this beautiful, braided rug

You will need:

2 bedcovers
(we used one full-size and one twin)
Scissors
Needle and thread
Pins
Tape measure
Sewing machine

1 Cut off all the hemmed sections of the bedcovers. Make snips into the fabric at 5cm (2in) intervals and tear long strips of fabric.

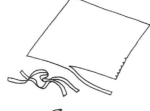

2 Taking three strips of fabric, hold them together at one end with the right sides facing up. Fold the ends to make the width narrower, as shown, and sew a line of stitching across the width to secure.

3 Place the sewn end under something heavy and plait the strips, keeping the plait even and fairly loose. When you reach the ends of the fabric strips, repeat Step 2 to secure with a line of stitching.

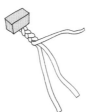

4 Once you have made several braided lengths in this way, take one of them and start coiling it to make a flat disk. Pin the coil together as you go and conceal the end of the plait to the back.

5 Turn the rug over and use large stitches to hand-sew the coils together. Keep the stitching to the back of your work, you don't need to take the needle through to the front. When you get to the last 10cm (4in) of a plaited strip, tuck this section to the back of the rug, at an angle so that it tapers in gradually. Secure the end of the plaited strip with a few stitches.

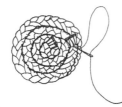

6 Start a new color by placing the braid 10cm (4in) back from the end of the first colour, just where it starts tapering in at the back of the rug. Pin the new strip in place and carry on coiling, keeping the circle shape as regular as possible. Repeat step 5 to finish each new strip.

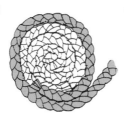

7 To make a scalloped section, you need to divide your braided strips into 17cm (6¾in) lengths. Starting from the stitched line at one end of a strip, measure 17cm (6¾in) along and stitch a new line. Leave a gap of 2cm (¾in) and stitch a second line, before measuring the next 17cm (6¾in) length. Continue in this way along the whole length of the strip. You can then cut the strip at the center of each 2cm (¾in) gap to create the lengths you need.

8 Pin the sections all around the edge of the rag rug, forming little semi-circles and tucking the raw edges underneath. Keep the scallop shapes as even as you can all around, adjusting them slightly to make them fit the circle. Make sure you keep the scallops even all the way around, or the circle will lose shape.

9 Secure each end of the semi-circle with some stitching. You can hand-sew this or use a sewing machine with a heavy-duty needle.

10 Work a new round of braided strips to enclose the scalloped section. Pin the braided strips to the tip of each semi-circle. Once you have completed a full circle, overlap the ends of the braided strips and sew together using a wide zig-zag stitch. Cut off any spare braid. Finish the circle by stitching the top of each semi-circle to the last round, to secure.

11 Repeat Steps 4 to 10 to build up the rug until you have the desired size, and finish with a final row of scallops.

Project taken from A Year in Crafts by Clare Youngs, published by CICO Books (£14.99). Photos © Joanna Henderson.

Starry sky Christmas

These luxurious festive stockings will bring seasonal glamour to any mantelpiece

You will need:

Scissors
50cm (20in) silk, 137cm (54in) wide, per stocking
Pins and sewing needle
40cm (16in) cotton batting (wadding),
for the lining
Star-shaped rubber stamp
Silver stamping ink

Sewing machine and matching thread
50cm (20in) silk velvet, 137cm (54in) wide,
for the cuff
Fabric glue
Small and medium-sized diamanté shapes
(for the stars and cuff)
Tassel with a hanging loop

stockings

1 Draw out a stocking shape on a piece of paper as a template. You want it to be roughly 44cm (17in) long by 23cm (9in) wide. Cut out the shape with scissors. Fold the silk fabric in half and pin the stocking template to the fabric to make a front and back. Cut through the two layers of fabric. Use the template again to cut out another stocking shape from the cotton batting (wadding).

2 Press the star stamp into the silver ink and stamp stars over one side of the stocking fabric, spaced approximately 5cm (2in) apart. Repeat on the other side of the stocking fabric if required. Allow the ink to dry completely.

3 With right sides of the silk fabric facing, pin the two stocking sections on top of the piece of cotton batting. Use the sewing machine with a matching thread to stitch through the three layers of fabric, leaving the top straight section of the stocking open.
  Trim and notch the curved edges of the fabric using the scissors.

4 Fold the silk velvet fabric in half lengthwise with the right sides facing. Pin and tack along the sides of the fabric and stitch together using the sewing machine. Turn to the right side.

5 Fold the velvet fabric in half with the velvet side facing the outside. Pin the fabric to the top of the silk stocking and hand stitch in place using small whipstitches. Turn the stocking right side out and fold the velvet cuff over the top of the stocking, keeping it in place with a few stitches.

6 Use the glue to stick a small diamanté decoration carefully to the center of each printed star on the stocking. Leave the glue to dry thoroughly.

7 Use the glue to stick the larger diamanté decorations, approximately 2cm (³/₄in) apart, around the bottom of the cuff. Leave to dry completely.

8 Hand stitch the tassel with the loop to the top of the stocking to finish before hanging up your stocking.

Project taken from Christmas Crafts by Catharine Woram, published by CICO Books (£12.99). Photos © Caroline Arber.

Phrase & Fable Quiz

Try your hand at this miscellany of questions about sayings and legends

1 What did the Bevin Boys do in the Second World War?
A: Direct traffic
B: Mine coal
C: Take minutes at meetings

2 The Queen referred to which year as her 'Annus horribilis', following a series of marital separations in the Royal Family, plus a fire at Windsor Castle?
A: 1992
B: 1994
C: 1996

3 If the cart were put before the horse, what would be happening?
A: Taking the horse for granted
B: Reversing of the natural order of things
C: Protecting the cart from bad weather

4 Which language do its speakers refer to as Ig-pay Atin-lay?
A: Pig Latin
B: Dog Latin
C: Fog Latin

5 Which other term was previously used to describe a Shotgun Wedding?
A: Abend Wedding
B: Garden Wedding
C: Knobstick Wedding

6 Who shot, with bow and arrow, an apple placed on the head of his own son?
A: William Wordsworth
B: William Shakespeare
C: William Tell

7 Which phrase did Eric Idle make famous in the late Sixties, deftly finished with 'say no more'?
A: Pink for winks
B: Nudge wink, top drawer
C: Nudge nudge, wink wink

8 If someone were 'completely crazy, or quite mad', what would they be?
A: As wrong as a mop
B: As dopey as a duster
C: As daft as a brush

9 The films Passport to Pimlico, Whisky Galore, Kind Hearts and Coronets and The Ladykillers are all examples of what?
A: Soho comedies
B: Ealing comedies
C: Brixton comedies

10 What does the acronym FAQ stand for?
A: Funny and queer
B: Fast and quick
C: Frequently asked questions

11 The 'agents of destruction', said to represent war, famine and pestilence are otherwise known as what?
A: The Four Horsemen of Doom
B: The Four Horsemen of Destruction
C: The Four Horsemen of the Apocalypse

12 If something will 'come out in the wash', what will it be?
A: Resolved
B: Ruined
C: Downsized

13 What are considered lucky, given that Mars (iron) is the enemy of Saturn (God of the Witches)?
A: Riding crops
B: Horseshoes
C: Saddles

14 Icarus did what, which would become his downfall?
A: Flew too close to the sun
B: Dived too deep in the ocean
C: Climbed too high in the wilderness

15 If someone lets the cat out of the bag, what have they done?
A: Run away from home
B: Disclosed a secret
C: Had a makeover

16 What food is said to have been provided 'from heaven' for the Israelites, during their journey from Egypt to the Holy Land?
A: Manna
B: Fish
C: Whelks

Q26: Do you remember Mr Humphreys' catchphrase?

Q9: Which famous film studio was responsible for The Ladykillers?

17 Who were Nippies, known for their nimbleness in the early Twentieth century?
A: Conductors
B: Waitresses
C: Seamstresses

18 What is the name of the beautiful queen in Swan Lake, and also of a French-born secret agent of the Second World War?
A: Manette
B: Odette
C: Suzette

19 Whose box reputedly set forth all the evils of the world when opened?
A: Venus's
B: Dido's
C: Pandora's

20 Pomfret cakes, made with liquorice since the 16th century are also known as what?
A: Welsh Cakes
B: Pontefract Cakes
C: Eccles Cakes

21 What are times of prosperity and happiness referred to as?
A: Dinard days
B: Halcyon days
C: Guinea days

22 Who in the army would be responsible for the stores and equipment?
A: Quartermaster
B: Base Colonel
C: Third Private

23 What became known as BBC English in the Twenties, due to the believed nature of its being most easily understood?
A: Regular Pronunciation
B: Renouned Pronunciation
C: Received Pronunciation

24 Who are you keeping up with, if you maintain a certain respect and status in social circles?
A: The Smiths
B: The Windsors
C: The Joneses

25 If someone has been 'sold down the river', what has happened?
A: A betrayal
B: An auction
C: An accident

26 What was TV's Mr Humphreys, whenever senior salesman Mr Peacock asked him to be?
A: Free
B: Prepared
C: Available

27 What was originally 'issued twice daily, as a quarter of a pint of rum with a pint of water', and was eventually banned in 1970 for all men and officers?
A: Grog
B: Smog
C: Mog

Turn to page 150 to see how you did

Inventions Quiz

Try your hand at this clever crop of questions about inventors and their creations

1 Benjamin Franklin began experiments in the late 18th century, which would lead to Thomas Edison inventing what almost 100 years later?
A: Firelight
B: Gas lighting
C: Electric lighting

2 What did Rolls Razor Limited produce in the Sixties, to the delight of many a housewife?
A: Washing machines
B: Magnifying mirrors
C: Electric hobs

3 Banjo-playing student dropout Richard Drew invented what in 1930, that would help us seal our wartime ammunition boxes?
A: Sticky tape
B: PVA glue
C: Plasters

4 Tim Berners-Lee is credited with inventing what international phenomenon in 1989?
A: Concorde
B: The World Wide Web
C: Climate change measurement

Q25: Which invention did Mrs Beeton urge housewives to buy?

5 What was invented by Percy Spencer, and initially called the Radarange when first sold in 1946?
A: Submarine
B: Electronic catapult
C: Microwave

6 William Howard Livens invented the first British what in 1924, designed to help out at home?
A: Dishwasher
B: Vacuum cleaner
C: Robo-butler

7 Sir Clive Sinclair created one of the world's cheapest home computers in 1982 – what was it called?
A: Spectrum Vega
B: ZX Spectrum
C: Sir Clive Spectrum

8 Central heating became a household must-have in the Seventies. Consequently the average room temperature has risen from 18°C in the Fifties to what today?
A: 20°C
B: 22°C
C: 26°C

9 Which Eastman Kodak camera range was extremely popular during the 20th century with its popular catchphrase, 'you push the button, we do the rest'?
A: Beaver
B: Guide
C: Brownie

10 Which modern gadget paved the way for other 'tablets', with the newest models including the Air, Air 2 and Mini?
A: iPad
B: Smartphone
C: Microsoft

11 What gadget revolutionised healthy cooking by using rapid air technology to ensure food is crispy on the outside without drying out?
A: HealthHob
B: Airfryer
C: Crisper

12 What began its life as a sticky white substance in the Seventies, but was changed when manufacturers feared children might mistake it for sweets?
A: Blu-Tack
B: Pritt Stick
C: No More Nails

13 The Kindle, Nook and Kobo Glo are called what, because of their ability to store books in electronic format?
A: Smartbooks
B: Smart readers
C: e-Readers

14 These days we use our phones for taking pictures, browsing the Internet and sending text messages. But in which decade was the first mobile phone call made?
A: Seventies
B: Eighties
C: Nineties

15 Hungarian newspaper editor Laszlo Biro invented what in the Thirties?
A: Readers' letters page
B: Rubber bands
C: Ballpoint pen

Q24: Can you name this record-breaking steam train?

16 The UK was the largest exporter of what in the Fifties, second only to America in their production, with the originals produced way back in the 1890s?
A: Balloons
B: Cars
C: Ice-cream

17 You can find them on most phones and computers, the Egyptians had their own version and earlier models were known as Arithmometers. What are they?
A: Calculators
B: Thermometers
C: Blood pressure monitors

18 What were the Underwood, Hammond and Remington? These machines helped many women into paid work for the first time, and the last UK model was built in 2012.
A: Tills
B: Diggers
C: Typewriters

19 St. Andrew's Paper Mill of Great Britain first introduced two-ply toilet paper in 1942. But what was the primary appeal of Northern Tissue, back in 1935?
A: It came on a roll
B: It was splinter-free
C: It was available in all Post Offices

20 The Americans were first to patent an affordable version of this household item. The first model was called the 'June Day', and powered by electricity or gas. What is it?
A: Tumble dryer
B: Ice-cream maker
C: Tanning machine

21 Lady Jennifer Bell invented the first of these back in 1912 – but what beauty appliance is now manufactured by famous brands including Remington, Hed Kandi and GHD?
A: Eyelash curler
B: Epilator
C: Hair straighteners

22 We now know this household appliance, invented by Englishman Hubert Cecil Booth in 1901, by its brand name. What is that name?
A: Windows
B: Smeg
C: Hoover

23 What did the BBC first broadcast in colour in 1967, prompting ITV to follow suit and regular colour broadcasting to be the norm by 1969?
A: Wimbledon
B: The Generation Game
C: Blue Peter

24 The first British steam trains was pioneered by Cornishman Richard Trevithick in 1804. But the record-breaking steam train, which reached 126mph in July 1938, was known as what?
A: Mallard
B: Pollard
C: Wellard

25 First brought to London's Great Exhibition in 1851, what did Mrs Beeton urge housewives to purchase, despite popular models still costing more than three times the weekly wage of a skilled workman?
A: Sewing machines
B: Pie funnels
C: Boot brushes

Turn to page 150 to see how you did

Q23: What was the BBCs first colour broadcast?

UK History Quiz

Travel through the centuries with our questions from the past

1 The Battle of Hastings took place in which year?
A: 1066
B: 1166
C: 1161

2 Scholars established which university in 1209?
A: Oxford
B: Cambridge
C: Durham

3 Robert the Bruce defeated Edward II at which battle in 1314?
A: Bannockburn
B: Wallace
C: York

4 What began on May 24, 1337?
A: The Great European Famine
B: The Black Death
C: The Hundred Years' War

5 Which famous work of literature by Geoffrey Chaucer came into the public domain in 1387?
A: Old Wives' Tales
B: Canterbury Tales
C: Tales with Mother

6 Owain Glyn Dwr led what, in the early 1400s?
A: The Irish expedition
B: The Welsh revolt
C: The Peasants' Revolt

7 The first Scottish university was founded in 1413. Which was it?
A: Glasgow University
B: King's College Aberdeen
C: St Andrews

8 What was unusual about Henry VI's accession to the throne in 1422?
A: She was actually a woman brought up as a man so she could rule
B: He was less than a year old at the time
C: He was crowned at York Minster due to revolts in the south

9 William Caxton did what for the first time in England, in 1477?
A: Published a printed book
B: Led a rebellion against taxes
C: Attended Royal Council despite being of common birth

10 The War of the Roses was decided by the defeat of Richard III by Henry Tudor at which battleground?
A: Bosworth
B: St Albans
C: Towton

11 In the early 16th century, King Henry VIII appealed to the Pope to do what?
A: Annul his marriage
B: Cease trade with Germany
C: Stop trade of false artifacts

Q11: What did King Henry VIII ask the Pope to do?

12 Katharine of Aragon, Henry VIII's first wife, died in January 1536. At which cathedral was she buried?
A: Canterbury
B: Peterborough
C: St Paul's

13 Henry VIII's first male heir, Edward, was born to which of his wives?
A: Anne of Cleeves
B: Katherine Parr
C: Jane Seymour

14 The Treaty of Edinburgh was signed in 1560, by which two countries?
A: England and France
B: England and Scotland
C: Scotland and France

15 The Gunpowder Plot to assassinate James I was uncovered on November 5 in which year?
A: 1599
B: 1605
C: 1628

Q1: When did the Battle of Hastings take place?

Q28: How many poppies were planted at the Tower of London?

16 Which famous diary writer began documenting their everyday life in 1660?
A: George Eliot
B: John Locke
C: Samuel Pepys

17 Who became our first Prime Minister in 1721?
A: Sir Robert Walpole
B: William Pitt
C: John Wesley

18 Nelson's Column famously stands in London's Trafalgar Square. But which Norfolk seaside town has been the proud home of Nelson's Monument since 1819?
A: Hunstanton
B: Cromer
C: Great Yarmouth

19 Which paper, first known as the Daily Universal Register, was first published in 1788?
A: The Daily Mail
B: The Times
C: The Observer

20 Who set up the Metropolitan Police in 1829, and lent his name to a well-known nickname for its employees?
A: Robert Robertson
B: Robert Peel
C: Robert Fuzz

21 Rowland Hill proposed a flat rate of what cost per stamp in 1840?
A: One farthing
B: One penny
C: Sixpence

22 What was founded by Charles Hallé in 1858?
A: Britain's first operatic society
B: Britain's first dramatic society
C: Britain's first symphony orchestra

23 Who wrote the popular novel, North and South, later serialised for TV?
A: Charles Dickens
B: George Eliot
C: Elizabeth Gaskell

24 Which Act was passed in 1871, which made seaside holidays ever more popular?
A: Bank Holiday Act
B: Road Traffic Act
C: Public Swimming Act

25 Education became compulsory for whom in 1880?
A: Children under five
B: Children under ten
C: Children with poor parents

26 Sir William Armstrong's home was the first to use electric lights in which year?
A: 1881
B: 1889
C: 1891

27 The Hackney Empire, a Grade II listed London theatre, has stood since 1901. But who designed it?
A: Frank Matcham
B: Isambard Kingdom Brunel
C: Ralph Erskine

28 How many ceramic poppies were planted at the Tower of London in 2014, to commemorate each of our fallen soldiers from The Great War?
A: 777, 246
B: 877, 246
C: 888, 246

Q24: Which Act of Parliament made seaside holidays popular?

Turn to page 150 to see how you did

Facts and figures

Here are some handy conversion tables for cooks

Dry weight

IMPERIAL	METRIC
½ oz	15 g
1 oz	25 g
2 oz	50 g
3 oz	75 g
4 oz	110 g
5 oz	150 g
6 oz	175 g
7 oz	200 g
8 oz	225 g
9 oz	250 g
10 oz	275 g
11 oz	300 g
12 oz	350 g
13 oz	375 g
14 oz	400 g
15 oz	425 g
1 lb	450 g
1 lb 2 oz	500 g
1 ½ lb	680 g
1lb 10oz	750 g
2 lb	900 g

Liquid

IMPERIAL	METRIC
½ fl oz	15 ml
1 fl oz	30 ml
2 fl oz	60 ml
3 fl oz	90 ml
5 fl oz (¼ pint)	150 ml
8 fl oz	225 ml
10 fl oz (½ pint)	300 ml
12 fl oz	350 ml
18 fl oz	500 ml
20 fl oz (1 pint)	600 ml
1 ¾ pints	1 litre
2 pints	1.25 litres
2 ½ pints	1.5 litres
3 ½ pints	2 litres

Other equivalents

Pinch	⅛ teaspoon
1 tablespoon	3 teaspoons
⅛ cup	2 tablespoons
¼ cup	4 tablespoons
⅓ cup	5 tablespoons plus 1 teaspoon
½ cup	8 tablespoons
1 cup	16 tablespoons or 8 fl oz

Oven temperatures

°C	°C with fan	°F	Gas Mark
110	90	225	¼
120/130	100/110	250	½
140	120	275	1
150	130	300	2
160/170	140/150	325	3
180	160	350	4
190	170	375	5
200	180	400	6
220	200	425	7
230	210	450	8
240	220	475	9

*Quantities aren't exact but have been calculated to give proportional measurements

Eat seasonably

All fruit and vegetables have a season – when they are better tasting and good value. Use our monthly table to guide you through what's in season and you'll be able to enjoy nature's produce at its very best

	JAN	FEB	MAR	APR	MAY	JUN	JUL	AUG	SEP	OCT	NOV	DEC
Apple									SEP	OCT	NOV	
Asparagus					MAY	JUN						
Beans (Broad)						JUN	JUL	AUG				
Beans (Runner)							JUL	AUG	SEP	OCT		
Beetroot	JAN						JUL	AUG	SEP	OCT	NOV	DEC
Blackberries									SEP	OCT		
Blackcurrants							JUL	AUG				
Blueberries							JUL	AUG	SEP			
Broccoli							JUL	AUG	SEP	OCT		
Brussels Sprout	JAN	FEB							SEP	OCT	NOV	DEC
Cabbage (Spring)	JAN	FEB	MAR	APR				AUG	SEP	OCT	NOV	DEC
Cabbage (White)									SEP	OCT	NOV	DEC
Cabbage (Savoy)	JAN	FEB	MAR				JUL	AUG	SEP	OCT	NOV	DEC
Cabbage (Red)								AUG	SEP	OCT	NOV	
Carrots	JAN	FEB				JUN	JUL	AUG	SEP	OCT	NOV	DEC
Cauliflower	JAN	FEB	MAR	APR	MAY		JUL	AUG	SEP	OCT	NOV	DEC
Celery							JUL	AUG	SEP	OCT		
Cherries							JUL	AUG				
Courgette						JUN	JUL	AUG	SEP			
Cucumber				APR	MAY	JUN	JUL	AUG	SEP			
Gooseberry						JUN	JUL	AUG				
Kale	JAN	FEB							SEP	OCT	NOV	DEC
Leeks	JAN	FEB	MAR						SEP	OCT	NOV	DEC
Lettuce (Cos)							JUL	AUG	SEP			
Lettuce (Curly)					MAY	JUN	JUL	AUG				
Lettuce (Iceberg)							JUL	AUG	SEP			
Marrow								AUG	SEP	OCT	NOV	DEC
Parsnip	JAN	FEB	MAR						SEP	OCT	NOV	DEC
Pears									SEP	OCT		
Peas						JUN	JUL	AUG	SEP			
Plums								AUG	SEP			
Potatoes (Maincrop)										OCT	NOV	DEC
Potatoes (New)				APR	MAY	JUN						
Pumpkin										OCT	NOV	DEC
Raspberries							JUL	AUG				
Redcurrant							JUL	AUG				
Rhubarb					MAY	JUN	JUL					
Spinach					MAY	JUN	JUL	AUG	SEP	OCT		
Strawberries						JUN	JUL	AUG				
Squash									SEP	OCT		
Sweetcorn								AUG	SEP	OCT		
Tomatoes						JUN	JUL	AUG	SEP	OCT		
Turnip	JAN	FEB								OCT	NOV	DEC
Watercress				APR	MAY	JUN	JUL	AUG	SEP			

Notable dates 2016

New Year's Day (Bank Holiday)	Friday January 1
Bank Holiday (Scotland)	Monday January 4
Epiphany	Wednesday January 6
Burns' Night	Monday January 25
Chinese New Year (Monkey)	Monday February 8
Shrove Tuesday (Pancake Day)	Tuesday February 9
Ash Wednesday	Wednesday February 10
Valentine's Day	Sunday February 14
St David's Day	Tuesday March 1
Mothering Sunday	Sunday March 6
Commonwealth Day	Monday March 14
St Patrick's Day (Bank Holiday N. Ireland/Eire)	Thursday March 17
Palm Sunday	Sunday March 20
Maundy Thursday	Thursday March 24
Good Friday (Bank Holiday)	Friday March 25
British Summer Time begins (clocks go forward)	Sunday March 27
Easter Sunday	Sunday March 27
Easter Monday (Bank Holiday)	Monday March 28
First Day of Passover (Jewish Holiday)	Saturday April 23
St George's Day	Saturday April 23
May Day (Early May Bank Holiday)	Monday May 2
Ascension Day	Thursday May 5
Armed Forces Day	Saturday May 21
Spring Bank Holiday	Monday May 30
First Day of Ramadan (Islam)	Monday June 6
Fathers' Day	Sunday June 19
Summer Solstice (Longest day)	Monday June 20
American Independence Day	Monday July 4
Battle of the Boyne (Holiday N. Ireland)	Tuesday July 12
St Swithun's Day	Friday July 15
Summer Bank Holiday (Scotland / Eire)	Monday August 1
Summer Bank Holiday	Monday August 29
Islamic New Year	Sunday October 2
Jewish New Year (Rosh HaShanah)	Monday October 3
Trafalgar Day	Wednesday October 21
British Summer Time ends (clocks go back)	Sunday October 30
Diwali (Hindu Festival)	Sunday October 30
Hallowe'en	Monday October 31
All Saints' Day	Tuesday November 1
Guy Fawkes' Night	Saturday November 5
Remembrance Sunday	Sunday November 13
First Sunday in Advent	Sunday November 27
St Andrew's Day	Wednesday November 30
Winter Solstice (Shortest day)	Monday December 21
CHRISTMAS DAY	Sunday December 25
BOXING DAY	Monday December 26
Bank Holiday (as Christmas falls on Sunday)	Tuesday December 27
New Year's Eve/Hogmanay	Saturday December 31

DIARY 2016

28 Monday

29 Tuesday

30 Wednesday

31 Thursday

1 Friday

2 Saturday

3 Sunday

Blast from the past

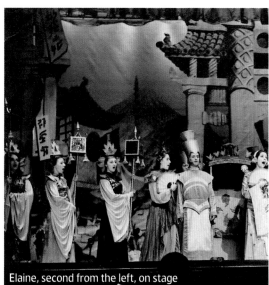

Elaine, second from the left, on stage

Blowing hot and cold

I was an unworldly 16 year old setting off on my first time away from home to join the Tiller Girls as 'Special Chorus' in an Emile Littler pantomime, Aladdin, with Nat Jackley playing Dame and Jimmy Clitheroe, Wishy Washy. My parents came to Euston to see me off and, promising my very worried mother I would write often, I boarded the train to Manchester, where I was welcomed into a private house and met the other five singers.

Given a weekend leave I eagerly travelled home. Feeling very sophisticated and grown up I dressed in black, wearing patent leather high heels and I had cut my hair. Quite a change for my mother to accept, but she didn't say a word. The journey back to Manchester was quite a different story – horrendously slow and very cold. My feet were freezing so I slipped my shoes off and put my feet on the hot bar that ran the length of the carriage. Arriving at 10pm, no matter how I squeezed I could not get my beautiful shoes back on and had to walk the length of the platform into a taxi on bare feet. So much for sophistication. Lesson learned!

Elaine Piesse, St Albans

What a good idea!

If your carpets and rugs have started to get a bit grubby or have a bit of a smell, you can freshen them up just using some bicarbonate of soda. Just sprinkle a thin layer of it over your rug or carpet, leave it to settle for 15 minutes, then vacuum it all up.

Sue Bourne, Stoke-on-Trent

Quick brain boost

Can you unscramble this anagram to make an 11-letter word?

EVADE RABBIT

Answer below

Garden inspiration

PIC: ALAMY

Jobs for late December

◆ Check houseplants for aphids and whitefly. Avoid over watering.
◆ Winter-prune fruit trees, removing all dead, damaged or diseased wood.
◆ Winter-prune wisteria.
◆ Avoid walking on frozen grass as this causes permanent damage.
◆ On a mild day, open the greenhouse windows to let some air in.
◆ When browsing through seed catalogues, be adventurous and order something you've never tried before.
◆ Take root cuttings from shrubs and dormant herbaceous perennials such as hollyhocks and Oriental poppies.
◆ Prune late-flowering clematis such as C Jackmanii.
◆ Protect celery with straw or bracken.

Senior moments

One night I woke up with an awful migraine so I reached out for the painkillers I keep on my bedside table, along with a glass of water and washed everything down. To my horror, the next morning, the tablets were still there next to the empty glass. That was six months ago and I still haven't found my lovely pearl earrings that went missing that same night. **Mrs E Temple, Londonderry**

Quick brain boost answer: Abbreviated

Recipe of the week

GNOCCHI BOLOGNESE WITH SPINACH

Serves: 4
Preparation time: 20 mins
Cooking time: 25 mins

2 tbsp olive oil
1 onion, finely chopped
450g (1lb) lean minced beef
700g (1lb 8oz) jar passata
Pinch of sugar
1 tbsp chopped fresh Italian herbs
450g (1lb) fresh spinach
1 garlic clove, crushed
500g packet fresh gnocchi
100g (4oz) mascarpone cheese
50g (2oz) freshly grated Parmesan cheese
Sea salt and freshly ground black pepper

1 Heat half the olive oil in a pan and tip in the onion and sauté for 2-3 mins until softened. Stir in the minced beef and cook for another few mins until lightly browned. Stir in the passata and add the sugar and herbs, season and simmer for 15-20 mins until slightly thickened.
2 Heat a large heavy-based pan and add fistfuls of the spinach, adding another as one wilts down. Cook for 1 min, then tip into a colander and gently press out any excess moisture.
3 Heat the rest of the olive oil in the pan and sauté the garlic for 30 seconds then add the drained spinach and season to taste. Toss until heated through.
4 When the sauce is almost ready, cook the gnocchi according to packet instructions and then tip into a colander to drain.
5 Mix the mascarpone with the Parmesan and season with pepper. Stir the gnocchi and spinach into the sauce and tip into a large ovenproof dish.
6 Add dollops of the mascarpone mixture and grill until bubbling and golden.
©www.simplybeefandlamb.co.uk

4	Monday

5	Tuesday

6	Wednesday

7	Thursday

8	Friday

9	Saturday

10	Sunday

Blast from the past

The big-freeze brought everything to a standstill

Big-freeze memories

During the big-freeze winter of 1962-63 I was teaching at Matthew Arnold school in Staines, Middlesex. After the snow, everything froze – including the River Thames (see photo). The coal ran out and so of course the school boilers went out and staff and pupils were sent home – with plenty of homework. Then every three or four days we would report in – trudging up to four miles through the frozen compacted snow to school. Wrapped in coats, gloves, scarves and boots we went to our allotted classrooms. Pupils signed in, bringing with them their sheets of written homework, which we took to mark and gave them out more to do. No one grumbled, all were happy to muck in and just exchange experiences. My father was a greengrocer and I'd be asked what, if any, fresh fruit and veg he had – so many foods were in short supply because of the weather. We were having a craft fair to raise money for hall curtains and I had charge of wools and silks, etc. Pupils collected materials and left completed items behind – done in either daylight or candlelight as many had no electricity.

Finally, after nearly four weeks, school was back to normal, the trains were running again and I was, at last, able to visit my cousins, over from South Africa who were staying in London. And although the snow meant many events were cancelled we did all manage to see the Boat Show at Olympia.

Mrs Priscilla Odell, Middx

What a good idea!

Use cooking salt to get rid of the stains in tea or coffee mugs. Simply sprinkle some salt on to a damp dishcloth and gently rub over the stained areas. Then give your mugs a rinse with warm water. This is much less toxic than using bleach and yet wonderfully effective.

Carol Cheetham, Birmingham

Quick brain boost

Can you solve this riddle?

He who makes it, has no need of it. He who buys it, has no use for it. He who uses it can neither see nor feel it.

Answer below

Garden inspiration

PIC: MARGARET WHITTAKER

Visit Alnwick Castle Garden

Take advantage of lower winter entrance prices to visit the unusual gardens of Alnwick Castle in Northumberland. Designed by Jacques and Peter Wirtz, the garden's dramatic centrepiece is the Grand Cascade. Water is a major theme throughout and the Serpent Garden features some impressive water sculptures. Pass through the Venetian Gates to discover a more traditional area, the formal Ornamental Garden. Children love the treetop walkways around the wooden treehouse restaurant while visitors of all ages enjoy looking out for red squirrels on the woodland walk.
**Visit www.alnwickgarden.com
or call 01665 511350**

Senior moments

I was just about getting to grips with my new laptop when a very confused looking lady suddenly appeared on the screen. I leaned in to take a closer look and was startled to see her doing the same. Then I realised that I had accidentally turned on my webcam and the lady on the screen was actually me.

Norma Jackson, Sussex

Quick brain boost answer: **A coffin**

Recipe of the week

APPLE & CAROM SEED CRUMBLE

Serves: 4
Preparation time: 10 mins
Cooking time: 25 mins

For the crumble topping:
120g (5oz) plain flour
60g (2^1/$_2$oz) caster sugar
1 tsp carom seeds
60g (2^1/$_2$oz) unsalted butter at room temperature, cut into pieces
For the fruit compote:
300g (10^1/$_2$oz) cooking apples
30g (1oz) unsalted butter
30g (1oz) demerara sugar
^{1}/$_4$ tsp ground cinnamon
100g (4oz) blackberries

1 Preheat oven to 190°C/375°F/Gas Mark 5.
2 To make the crumble, tip the flour and sugar into a large bowl. Add the carom seeds and butter, and then rub into the flour using your fingertips to make a light breadcrumb texture. Sprinkle the mixture evenly in a thin layer over a baking sheet and bake for 12-15 mins.
3 For the compote, peel, core and cut the apples into 2cm (^{3}/$_4$in) dice. Put the butter and sugar into a medium saucepan and melt together over a medium heat. Cook for 3 mins until the mixture turns to a light caramel colour. Stir in the apples and cook for a further 3 mins. Add the cinnamon, stir and cook for another 3 mins.
4 Cover the pan with a lid, remove from the heat, then leave for 2-3 mins to continue cooking in the warmth of the pan. Sprinkle in the blackberries. Spoon the warm fruit into an oven-proof gratin dish and top with the crumble mix, then reheat in the oven for 5-10 mins.

©Spice at home by Vivek Singh, published by Absolute Press.

January 11 -17

11 Monday

12 Tuesday

13 Wednesday

14 Thursday

15 Friday

16 Saturday

17 Sunday

Blast from the past

Freshly-baked bread was delivered to the door

Delivering bread in Devon

When I was a child we lived in a small (and at that time) rural Devonshire village. As you can imagine, precious Saturday jobs were very few and far between and so my weekly extra pocket money came from helping on a bread round. Our next-door neighbour, Dorothy, worked for a local shop owned by Percy and Hilda. Percy was the local baker and this meant that every Saturday morning a wooden handcart, with a hinged half-hoop lid, would be loaded with bread and all the other goodies he had freshly made. Then Dorothy would push the cart all around the village with me going alongside delivering orders door to door. The cart stood six foot high when the lid was opened and was around six to seven feet long (I'm the taller girl at the back in the photo). Its wheels were about three foot high.

How much did I earn? I can't really remember but I think it would have been around five shillings.

During the winter there were times when one got bitterly cold, so to arrive home and be met with hot cocoa and the fire-door of our Rayburn opened to warm me was more than welcome.

When no longer in use the cart was decorated and left on display outside the shop until sadly it was stolen.

One of the baker's grandchildren now lives in the USA and it was lovely to see on Facebook recently a loaf she had made using her granddad's recipe and tin.

Janice Bawler, Devon

What a good idea!

I was having trouble threading a needle the other day. So I had the idea to spray the end of the thread with a little cheap hairspray. This makes the cotton go stiff and makes it so much easier to thread the needle. It's worked every time since for me – hooray for no more squinting at tiny needle eyes!

Freda Fimmenty, Essex

Garden inspiration

PIC: ALAMY

Great garden tip

Throughout the year, take photos of different aspects of your garden so you have a ready reference showing what is in bloom and when. This is particularly useful if you have a mixed herbaceous border that also has spring bulbs in it. It's surprising how quickly we forget from one season to the next! Photos taken in March, April and May indicating where crocuses, daffodils and tulips are planted help to prevent them being accidentally dug up when putting in new plants or more bulbs later in the year.

Senior moments

I'm a school welfare lady and one day I asked a little girl at school what she had got for her birthday. "I got a black beret," she replied. "Ooh good," I said, "that should keep you warm all through winter." She looked a bit bewildered. "No, it's a phone, Miss" she said, "a Blackberry."

Mrs M Sowerby, Nottingham

Recipe of the week

GRIDDLED SALMON & CHILLI STIR FRY

Serves: 4
Preparation time: 10 mins
Cooking time: 15 mins

4 salmon fillets
300g (10$^{1}/_{2}$oz) long-stemmed broccoli
12 shallots, peeled and quartered
1 large red chilli, finely chopped
50g (2oz) almonds, toasted

1 Brush the salmon steaks with a little oil, griddle or pan fry for approximately 5–7 mins each side until cooked through, keep warm.
2 Steam the broccoli for 2 min, drain well. Heat the clean griddle pan, toss the shallots in a little oil and cook, turning regularly, until softened and beginning to brown at the edges.
3 Add the chilli to a tablespoon of olive oil and toss into the broccoli, add to the pan and cook with the shallots until just beginning to show griddle marks, turning at regular intervals. Sprinkle in the toasted almonds.
4 Divide the stir fry between 4 plates and top with a piece of salmon.
© www.ukshallot.com

18 Monday

19 Tuesday *my best friends killed herself on this day*

20 Wednesday

21 Thursday

22 Friday

23 Saturday

24 Sunday

Blast from the past

Colette shared a bedroom with her brothers and sisters

Sardines in a can

I grew up in the Fifties in Lurgan, Northern Ireland, and our house had a small living room, a dining room and a very small scullery or kitchen. Washing was done in a large sink in the scullery and Mammy used the old-fashioned scrubbing-board and a bar of Lifebuoy soap. There was no hot running water, so it had to be heated up first on the large gas cooker and then poured into the sink. With 12 of us, there were huge loads of washing to be done and poor Mammy was kept very busy! The clothes had to be hung out to dry on lines in a very small backyard, a bit at a time.

Upstairs there were two bedrooms. Mammy and Daddy used one room along with the youngest baby. The rest of us children shared the other bedroom: girls in one bed and boys in the other. It was like sardines in a can. Frequently we wrestled over the blankets, some of which had sleeves, pockets and buttons! Each night at bedtime Mammy would bring the younger children upstairs first. Then a couple of hours later the older children would go up the stairs very quietly with the first in line carrying the Wee Willie Winkie type candlestick with a lit candle to guide our way. We had a chamber pot under the bed so that we didn't have to struggle down the stairs in the dark to the outside toilet. I don't remember any of us trying to jump the queue to empty it in the mornings!

Colette Turner, N Ireland

Quick brain boost

Can you crack the code? If D=A, H=E and U=R what does UHIULJHUDWRU say?

Answer below

Garden inspiration

PIC: ALAMY

Jobs for January

◆ Plant bare-root peonies and roses as they are cheaper and more vigorous than pot-grown plants.
◆ Tackle tap-root weeds by pushing a bulb planter down to remove the tap-root as well the leaves. Fill the hole with compost.
◆ Check stored dahlias for signs of rot. Cut out the affected part, wrap the tuber in newspaper and replace in storage.
◆ Onion seeds can be started now ready to be planted out at the end of March.
◆ Sow sweet peas in deep pots for early flowering. Plant bare-root peonies and roses as they are cheaper and more vigorous than pot-grown plants.

Senior moments

One of my neighbours goes to the community centre every day for his lunch. But one day he was put on a different table to usual and not knowing any of the other diners, he introduced himself. "I'm Geoff," he said, turning to the lady next to him. "So am I" replied the lady, "but I'm usually all right if I've got my hearing aid in". **Connie Fisher, Enfield**

What a good idea!

Here are some top tips for other knitters. When you are knitting with white wool, lightly dust your hands with talcum powder first to keep the wool nice and clean. If you're knitting with darker wools, first cover your lap with a white cloth. This will stop your eyes straining to see the wool as much. **Audrey Moon, Mablethorpe**

Quick brain boost answer: Refrigerator (each letter is shifted 3 letters down the alphabet)

Recipe of the week

NAAN BREAD PIZZA

Serves: 2
Preparation time: 10 mins
Cooking time: 10–12 mins

2 plain naan bread
2 tbsp flatleaf parsley, chopped
1 tbsp capers, roughly chopped
1 small garlic clove, finely chopped
1 tbsp olive oil
180g (6oz) pack Sweet Chilli Beetroot, cut into wedges
55g (2¼oz) pepperoni
1 x 125g(4½oz) ball mozzarella, torn into pieces
Freshly ground black pepper

1 Preheat the oven to 220°C/430°F/Gas Mark 7.
2 Arrange the naan on a baking sheet.
3 In a small bowl, mix together the parsley, capers, garlic and oil, then divide between the naan and spread all over with the back of a spoon.
4 Top each naan evenly with the Sweet Chilli Beetroot, pepperoni, and mozzarella.
5 Grind over a little black pepper and bake in the hot oven for 10–12 mins until the naan is crisp and the cheese is melted. Serve immediately.

©www.lovebeetroot.co.uk

25 Monday

26 Tuesday

27 Wednesday

28 Thursday

29 Friday

30 Saturday

31 Sunday

Blast from the past

Dreaming of Olwen

The first record-player I remember was my dad's wind-up model. It sat on top of a cabinet that held his collection of piano rolls for a pianola. His choice of records began with Peter Dawson singing The Floral Dance on a heavy HMV 12-inch. I'll never forget rushing downstairs each morning to play my first record on the wind-up, The Dream of Olwen from the film, While I Live, on the Columbia label. There was even more excitement when the radiogram arrived – a huge piece of furniture that seemed to fill the front room of our end-of-terrace.

As I got older, the record I played over and over was Eddie Fisher and Outside of Heaven – I loved his velvety voice, although I also enjoyed Bing Crosby. By then I was learning to play the piano and records by Charlie Kunz, Semprini and Winifred Atwell came on the scene to inspire me. I also bought and loved The Happy Wanderer by the Obernkirchen Children's Choir and Count Your Blessings by the Luton Girls' Choir. They were both so popular then. Once I was married with young children – making up bottles and changing nappies – I had no spare cash any more for discs, so I swapped to listening on the radio. But those early records stay with me and I can still hear them in my head.

Barbara Bignell, Northants

What a good idea!

Washing up gloves have a tendency to smell a bit funny and make your hands smell rubbery for the rest of the day. So I now rub a few drops of essential oils, such as tea tree or lavender, into my rubber gloves. This leaves both my gloves and my hands smelling lovely all day.

Irene Thompson, Berkshire

Quick brain boost

Garden inspiration

PIC: ALAMY

In bloom now: fragrant honeysuckle

Planted by a door or near a path, winter-flowering
honeysuckle fills the chilly January air with
welcome perfume. Also known as shrubby
honeysuckle, Lonicera purpusii 'Winter Beauty'
bears creamy white tubular flowers on bare stems
from December to March. The blooms are followed
by bright green leaves. For best results, a third of
the flowering shoots should be removed after the
flowers have died. Cyclamen coum albissimum
'Golan Heights' (which is not widely available, but
can be grown from seed) would make the perfect
planting companion for this delightful shrub.

Senior moments

I always take my mobile to the theatre in case of
emergencies. So I was surprised when, rummaging
through my handbag to turn my phone off before the
show, I found that I'd put the TV remote in my bag
instead of my mobile. My daughter was later worried
why I hadn't answered any of her texts– I didn't dare
confess what I'd done.

Megan Greenwood, Manchester

Quick brain boost answer: Abnormality

Recipe of the week

HOMITY PIE

Serves: 6-8
Preparation time: 10 mins
Cooking time: 35 mins

375g (13oz) shortcrust pastry
400g (14oz) potatoes
2 hard-boiled eggs, peeled and quartered
4 small medium onions
60g (2½oz) butter
2 cloves garlic
1 stalk of thyme
150ml (5floz) double cream
100g (4oz) cheddar cheese
1 tsp mustard powder
Salt and pepper

1 Preheat oven to 200°C/400°F/Gas Mark 6.
2 Roll out the pastry and line a 25.5cm (10in) pie or
   tart case. Bake blind for 20 mins.
3 Boil the potatoes until tender and then chop into
   small cubes.
4 While the potatoes are boiling, melt the butter in a
   pan, add the thyme and slowly soften the onions
   and garlic.
5 Add the cubed potato, chopped eggs and grated
   cheese to the onions and then add the cream,
   mustard powder and salt and pepper.
6 Pour into the pastry case and cook for a further
   15 mins until the top is golden

©www.facebook.com/EggsForSoldiers

1 Monday

2 Tuesday

3 Wednesday

4 Thursday

5 Friday

6 Saturday

7 Sunday

Blast from the past

Brenda looking like Doris Day in 1966 and, below, in 1989

Doris is on the bus!

As a teenager I would see all the Doris Day films and think how I would like to look like her. Funnily enough, when I was 17 I lightened my hair and from that day forward people would remark how much like Doris I looked. When I was in my twenties I emigrated to America with my husband and two young children and there again people would come up to me and ask for my autograph. The bank I worked for as a secretary even asked me to go in for the Doris Day look-alike competition, but I refused as I was so shy in those days.

While on my way to work one morning a very funny incident happened. As I went to sit down at the front of the bus, a man sitting at the back excitedly turned to his wife and said: "Look, Doris Day has just got on the bus." "What's she doing riding on a bus?" queried his wife. "I don't know," the man snapped back, "she can ride on a bus if she wants to. Perhaps, she wants a change from riding in a car!" The next morning when I boarded the bus, the man was sitting on his own. He leaned over to the passenger nearest to him and said: "Did you notice Doris Day has just got on the bus?" I should have told the poor man he had made a mistake but I didn't, I just sat there enjoying the feeling of what it must be like to be a famous film star.

Brenda Smith, South Benfleet, Essex

Quick brain boost

Can you solve this riddle?

Paul is an assistant at a butcher's shop. He is six foot tall and wears size nine shoes. What does he weigh?

Answer below

Garden inspiration

Great garden tip

To keep expensive stainless steel garden tools such as spades, forks and hoes in good-as-new condition, they need to be thoroughly cleaned after use. A traditional way of doing this is to have a large bucket of builders' sand that has been mixed with sump oil close to the shed door. After wiping the worst of the soil off with a rag, plunge the tool up and down in the sand to complete the process, leaving a thin skin of protective oil on the metal during storage.

Senior moments

As my wife and I lay in bed recently, she said to me: "My memory isn't getting any better." I said: "Why, what have you forgotten now?" "Nothing," she replied, "it's just I thought it'd be better by now." I lay there bemused and said: "What on earth are you talking about?" "Well, these new pillows I bought said 'Improved Memory Pillows' but they don't seem to be working." Words fail me! **Ashley Howard, Hull**

What a good idea!

A pretty tea towel makes the perfect bag in which to keep all your spare plastic carrier bags. Just join the long sides of the tea towel together and sew together. Then make a hem at the top and the bottom using some elastic. Finally, add some strong ribbon to the top so it can hang on a door handle. **Ms Brown, Pickering**

Quick brain boost answer: Meat

Recipe of the week

CHOCOLATE FRIDGE CAKE

Serves: 10
Preparation time: 15 mins
Chilling time: 3 hours

200g (7oz) dark chocolate, broken into pieces
50g (2oz) butter
2 tbsp golden syrup
175g (6oz) good shortbread biscuits, roughly broken into pieces
50g (2oz) pistachio nuts, roughly chopped
175g (6oz) raspberries
150g (5oz) blueberries
75g (3oz) white chocolate, melted

1. Line a 20cm (8in) shallow square cake tin with baking paper.
2. Add the dark chocolate, butter and golden syrup to a bowl set over a saucepan of gently simmering water and heat for about 5 mins, stirring until melted.
3. Take the bowl off the heat, add all the biscuits and, keeping a few nuts and berries back for the top, stir the rest into the chocolate mix. Spoon into the tin and press into an even layer. Sprinkle with the remaining nuts and fruit. Chill for 3 hours until firm.
4. To finish, drizzle the melted white chocolate over the top of the cake in zigzag lines using a spoon, then chill for an extra 30 mins until set.

© www.seasonalberries.co.uk

8 Monday

9 Tuesday

10 Wednesday

11 Thursday

12 Friday

13 Saturday

14 Sunday

Blast from the past

Jenny (standing far left) at a hospital prize-giving in 1969

A nurse in the making

I left school at 16 in 1965 and became a pre-nursing student, working at a Bristol hospital, including Saturday mornings, and attending college two days a week. On our first day we all felt proud wearing our uniforms, including our white starched aprons and caps as we went to see Matron. However, she quickly pointed out that caps and aprons were only to be worn on Tuesdays at college – but she was very sweet about it and said how smart we all looked. We spent time on different wards making beds and making sure we did the envelope corners properly (which I still do at home to this day). We put laundry away, cleaned the sluices and in the nursery helped feed and change babies as well as generally looking after the sick children. Of all the wards, the children's was my favourite, although I also learned a lot working with the dietician in the hospital kitchens. I then went on to be a pupil nurse – a two-year course that I hoped would lead to me becoming a State Enrolled Nurse. And after regular weekly classes and gaining much more practical experience on the wards I gained my hospital certificate and badge. I enjoyed all aspects of my training – and went on to be very happy as a nurse. **Jenny Broe, Bristol**

What a good idea!

Don't be tempted to throw away the leftover crumbs that you get in the bottom of your cereal packet. Instead save them in an airtight jar and store this in your kitchen. These crumbs will come in ever so handy for scattering over meat stews or to use on top of a fruit crumble. **Maureen Hampton, Leicester**

Quick brain boost

What comes next in this number sequence?

1, 1, 2, 4, 7, 13, 24, ??

Answer below

Garden inspiration

PIC: TAMSYN WILLIAMS

Visit The Eden Project

Who doesn't dream of wandering in warmer climes at this chilly time of the year? This is the perfect month to seek the shelter of The Eden Project's world-famous domed conservatories. Spectacularly situated in a disused china clay quarry near St Austell in Cornwall, this vast botanical park offers visitors the opportunity to stroll through groves of olive and lemon trees in the Mediterranean Biome or swelter in the steamy heat as they trek through jungle in the Rainforest Biome.

Visit www.edenproject.com or call 01726 811911

Senior moments

I was recently shaping my eyebrows with some tweezers when I found one particular hair just refused to budge. I kept tugging at it, but to no avail. So I got out my magnifying mirror and turned on a bright light at which point I realised why I was having so much trouble – I was trying to pull out a wrinkle!

Pamela Lund, Fife

Quick brain boost answer: 44 (add the three previous numbers)

Recipe of the week

CHOCOLATE ORANGE PANCAKES

Serves: 4
Preparation time: 5 mins
Cooking time: 30 mins

60g (2^{1}/$_{2}$oz) wholemeal flour
120g (4^{1}/$_{2}$oz) self-raising flour
2 tsp baking powder
1 medium egg beaten
300ml (10^{1}/$_{2}$floz) skimmed milk
4 tbsp thin cut orange marmalade
30g (1oz) dark chocolate chips

1 Combine the two flours, baking powder, egg and milk and whisk to a smooth batter.
2 In a small saucepan, warm the marmalade until it becomes runny.
3 Stir the chocolate chips into the batter along with half of the marmalade.
4 Wipe a little vegetable or sunflower oil over the base of a large, heavy-based, non-stick frying pan and put on a medium heat.
5 Pour 2 tbsp of batter mixture into the pan and let it spread into a circle. Cook until you see bubbles rising and the top begins to set.
6 Flip over and cook the other side until brown. Cook 3 or 4 at a time depending on the size of your pan. Once cooked, keep warm on a plate under a folded tea towel while you cook the next batch.
7 Add 2 tsp of water to the remaining marmalade and reheat. Serve 3 or 4 in a stack drizzled with warm marmalade.
©www.streamlinefoods.co.uk

15 Monday

16 Tuesday

17 Wednesday

18 Thursday

19 Friday

20 Saturday

21 Sunday

Blast from the past

A visit to the dentist provided an enduring memory

A present from Dad

Shortly after the war began my father was called up as he had been in the army and was still on the reserve list. Just before my 11th birthday in 1940 I was due to have a tooth out at the local school dentist on a Saturday. I was petrified to go on my own but my mother, who was working by then, had to do the weekly shop. Then a miracle happened. My dad came home on unexpected leave and said he would take me.

I had the tooth out and, boy, did the gas make me feel ill. Dad carried me home and I was laid on the sofa with a blanket over me and fell fast asleep. When I woke up there was a bunch of bluebells on the pillow beside me. It seems that a gypsy had come to the door selling them and my dad had bought me a bunch to cheer me up. My dad died in 1959, but although I am now in my 85th year I have never forgotten him or his kind gesture so many years ago. He was one of the kindest dads any child would be proud of. He was my hero.

Mrs B Wyatt, Chester

What a good idea!

If you've been doing crafts, you might find that your scissors have become sticky with the residue from sellotape and glue. To clean them, just soak a cotton wool pad or tissue in some nail polish remover and wipe down the scissor hands with this. All the stickiness will go and your scissors will last much longer. **Mrs E Taylor, Aberdeen**

Quick brain boost

Can you crack the code?
If H=S, N=M and I=R what does KIRNILHVH say?

Answer below

Garden inspiration

PIC: ALAMY

Jobs for February

◆ Sow salad seeds such as salad rocket and hardy lettuces.
◆ Sow half-hardy annual climbers such as Ipomoea for early summer flowering
◆ Put mouse traps down in the greenhouse to prevent mice damaging newly-sown seeds.
◆ Prune winter-flowering shrubs such as mahonias or viburnums.
◆ Plant begonia tubers in a frost-free place such as a greenhouse for summer bedding or hanging baskets.
◆ Cut back dead foliage on perennials to make room for new growth. Divide older plants.
◆ Deadhead winter-flowering pansies to encourage more flowers.
◆ In a frost-free spell, plant gooseberry and currant bushes.

Senior moments

When I was writing out my shopping list for the day, I reminded my husband that we needed to buy a spare set of keys for the greenhouse and the shed. At this, I heard him open the fridge. "No, it's all right," he replied, "we have plenty to last until the weekend." He thought I'd said 'cheese' not 'keys'.

H Davies, Chesterfield

Quick brain booster answer: Primroses
(the letters in the alphabet are reversed)

Recipe of the week

CREAMY PASTA BAKE

Serves: 4
Prep time: 20 mins
Cooking time: 20 mins

375g (13oz) dried pasta shapes
1 onion, finely chopped
50g (2oz) unsalted butter
1 clove garlic, crushed
2 tbsp plain flour
450ml (15floz) milk
150ml double cream
150g (5oz) Cheddar, grated
200g (7oz) piece smoked ham, torn into shreds
Small bunch chives, snipped
Salt & freshly ground black pepper
500g (1lb1oz) cooked beetroot

1 Preheat the oven to 180°C/350°F/Gas Mark 4.
2 Cook pasta according to packet instructions. Drain and reserve.
3 Set a heavy-based saucepan over a low heat, sweat the onion in the butter for 10–15 mins until it starts to soften. Add the garlic and fry for a further minute before stirring through the flour.
4 Pour in milk and cream, and bring up to the boil, stirring constantly until thickened. Simmer steadily for 2–3 mins to cook the flour.
5 Turn off the heat, stir through half the cheese, the ham and chives. Season to taste with salt and freshly-ground black pepper.
6 Stir through the cooked pasta and beetroot and spoon into a baking dish. Scatter over the rest of the cheese and bake for about 20 mins until golden brown and bubbling.

©www.godminster.com

22 Monday

23 Tuesday

24 Wednesday

25 Thursday

26 Friday

27 Saturday

28 Sunday

Blast from the past

Not my happiest time

It has been said that schooldays are the happiest days of your life. Initially it was not so in my case, for I attended a prep school at the age of four in Exeter during the Second World War. The school was named Fairpark and was run by a Miss Butt. She was a large lady and very strict. When she spoke her voice seemed to boom – sufficient to quieten or scare the average school infant. If a child was late arriving there was certain to be a scolding. Clean hankies had to be exhibited every morning before class commenced.

Due to her strictness I did not enjoy attending school. It did not help that unfortunately I suffered with acidosis so therefore my third of a pint of milk (allocated to all children then) needed to be poured into a saucepan and brought to the boil to take off the cream. I think Miss Butt strongly begrudged this. The only way we children could take out our resentment at her behaviour was when she attempted to go through a doorway into the next class. This action required her to go sideways and when her back was turned we would giggle! We weren't so cheerful when she would cane the whole class with a tin ruler across the thumb if talking commenced after being told to be silent. Needless to say, I was so pleased at seven years of age when my parents decided to send me to a different school.

Sheila Mills, Minehead, Somerset

What a good idea!

This is a great natural anti-ageing tip. Put some pineapple juice in an ice tray and let it freeze overnight. The next day, take out one of these ice cubes and rub it over clean skin, wait for five minutes and then rinse your face. The enzymes in pineapple help make your skin feel more elastic and help stop skin getting dry. **Kauser Parveen, Derby**

Quick brain boost

Can you unscramble this anagram to make an 11-letter word?

LAZY HAD HARP   Answer below

Garden inspiration

In bloom now: elegant snowdrops

Growing wild in woodland and under roadside hedges, as well as in our gardens, snowdrops brighten the gloomy days of February with their pale beauty. The native snowdrop, Galanthus nivalis, is the easiest to naturalise and looks especially lovely when grown under trees with drifts of early-blooming Crocus tommasinianus 'Whitewell Purple'. For snowdrop enthusiasts, there are a bewildering number of cultivars to grow, ranging from aristocratic 'Lady Beatrix Stanley' to the early, long-stemmed 'Atkinsii' and 'Carolyn Elwes', an unusual yellow snowdrop that has the reputation of being 'difficult'.

Senior moments

I was in a hurry to go out so I quickly spritzed my hair. I thought it smelled a bit different and couldn't understand why my hair hadn't gone stiff. I then realised that I'd sprayed my hair with shoe polish rather than hairspray! Both were in green cans in the same cupboard. Now I know why my suede shoes went shiny.   **Patricia Clough, Kent**

Quick brain boost answer: Haphazardly

Recipe of the week

SPINACH, FETA & PINE NUT OMELETTE

Serves: 1
Preparation time: 5 mins
Cooking time: 5 mins

2 eggs
100g (4oz) bag of baby spinach, washed
30g (1¼oz) feta cheese, diced fairly small
1 tbsp toasted pine nuts
½ tbsp olive oil or coconut oil

1 Heat the oil in a small non-stick frying pan
2 Add the spinach and allow it to wilt in the heat of the pan – this will take about 3 minutes.
3 Add the beaten eggs and mix everything around in the pan.
4. As soon as the eggs start to set, tip in the feta cheese and the pine nuts. Continue turning everything around in the pan for a minute or so.
5 Leave the pan on the heat until the outside is starting to go a golden brown colour.
6 Place a plate over the pan and hold it down securely. Lift the pan and turn it over so that the omelette is on the plate.
7 Slide the omelette back into the pan and cook the other side, then serve when ready.
©www.eggrecipes.co.uk

29 Monday

1 Tuesday

2 Wednesday

3 Thursday

4 Friday

5 Saturday

6 Sunday

Blast from the past

Leaving sunny Australia

A chilly reception

In September 1954, my mum and dad went to Australia on the £10 passage, with us three children on the ship the Castle Felice. There were more than 2,000 people on board – we must have been like sardines in a can. We lived in Bald Hills, near Brisbane for eight years, until January 1962 when Mum and Dad made up their minds to come back to England (now with four children). When we left Australia it was sunny and hot but, six weeks later in March 1962, little did we know that we would come back to a freezing cold England, one of the coldest winters on record. We only had a few bits of clothing and I only had one coat. What a shock the cold and snow was – it went right through our bones. We children had never seen snow or ice before and actually had great fun.

And we all had to live in a caravan until Dad could get his money transferred from Australia, which took a very long time then. Mum had to ask friends for clothes and visit the charity shop. Luckily for us we were made of hard stuff and survived. When my aunt returned from Australia the following year – 1963 – she had the same thing too!

Mrs Laura Rickards, Bristol

What a good idea!

It can be difficult to clean into the nooks and crannies of your blinds. But I've found an easy solution. Just wrap a measuring ruler in a duster that's slightly damp and then slide this forwards and backwards across each of the slots in the blind. This will get rid of all the dust that's settled there.

Angela Tarren, Lincolnshire

Quick brain boost

Can you solve this riddle?

What belongs to you but others use it more than you do?

Answer below

Garden inspiration

PIC: SHUTTERSTOCK

Great garden tip

While out walking, take a pair of secateurs to cut twiggy sticks that can be used to support herbaceous plants later in the year (hazels are good for this purpose). Also save suitable branches from shrubs (cotinus, lilac, cotoneaster, sambucus) and trees (apples and pears) that require winter pruning. Another way of helping floppy plants such as catmint to stay upright is to put a wire hanging basket upside down over them while they are still dormant so that in the spring the shoots will be supported.

Senior moments

My husband took me to collect my car from the garage after it had been for a service. As I got to my car, I found that I couldn't unlock the door. "It won't budge," I said to my husband, as he was about to drive off. "What shall I do?" "Try opening the right car," he replied. "Yours is the green one in front."

Pauline Stott, Cardiff

Quick brain boost answer: Your name

Recipe of the week

CARROT CAKE

Serves: 6-8
Preparation time: 30 mins
Cooking time: 50 mins

150g (5oz) light brown sugar
150ml (¹/₄pt) vegetable oil
3 large eggs, beaten
150g (5oz) self-raising flour, sifted
1 tsp ground cinnamon
1 tsp bicarbonate of soda
250g (9oz) carrots, peeled and grated
100g (4oz) raisins
100g (4oz) vanilla yogurt
Frosting:
200g (8oz) soft cheese
75g (3oz) icing sugar
75g (3oz) vanilla yogurt

1 Preheat the oven to 180°C/350°F/Gas Mark 4. Grease and line a 18cm (7in) round loose-bottom tin.
2 Using a mixer with a balloon whisk, whisk the sugar with the vegetable oil and then gradually add in the eggs.
3 Fold in the flour, cinnamon and bicarbonate of soda. Add the carrots, raisins and yogurt and mix thoroughly.
4 Tip the mixture into the prepared tin and bake for 40-50 mins until firm to touch. Insert a skewer into the centre of the cake and if it comes out clean the cake is cooked. Transfer to a cooling rack.
5 To make the frosting, beat the soft cheese with the icing sugar and yogurt until smooth.
6 Decorate the cake with the frosting using a knife or the back of a spoon and spread to the sides. Transfer to a serving plate and slice.

© www.rachelsorganic.co.uk

7 Monday

8 Tuesday

9 Wednesday

10 Thursday

11 Friday

12 Saturday

13 Sunday

Blast from the past

Double wedding in the snow

I always remember, as a child, seeing the beautiful white dress in my mother's wardrobe and would listen to her story of her wedding day. My mother, Joan, was born seconds ahead of her identical twin, Mary Isabel, the eldest of seven children. They lived through hard times and did everything together. When, after the war, they each met their prospective husbands, Harold and Wilfred, they decided on a double wedding. This was a major problem for my nana, as rationing was in place in 1947. She saved, begged and exchanged coupons, scrimped and scrapped, and managed to provide double wedding dresses, bridesmaid dresses, flowers, wedding cakes, and food, plus photographer!

The wedding was planned to take place at the Holy Trinity Church in North Ormesby, near Middlesbrough, on March 15, 1947.

However, 1947 was the worst winter for many years, with heavy snowfall and drifting. On the day of the wedding, there had been more snow falling and the church pathway was covered by a couple of feet of snow. Family and friends had to dig out the pathway to the church for the wedding party, but everyone got stuck in and helped. My mother and Auntie Mary arrived looking beautiful, two lovely young women, looking forward to their new lives with their partners.

The story was also featured in the local paper. Every time there are news programmes about the weather we've had in Britain, they always show the winter of 1947 and it reminds me of the stories my mother told me of her wedding day.

Pam Smailes, Teesside

What a good idea!

When you're using a paint roller to emulsion your walls, line your tray first with cling film. This saves you a lot of washing up later as you can just pull off the cling film and throw the mess away. You can also wrap up your roller in cling film if you know you need to use it another day to add a second coat.

Janet Walton, Sheffield

Quick brain boost

Garden inspiration

PIC: MIKE WERKMEISTER

Visit East Lambrook Manor

Snowdrop lovers make a pilgrimage to admire the 80 varieties of their favourite plant blooming in this pretty Somerset garden created by Margery Fish in the Forties and Fifties. Since her death in 1969, several rare varieties of snowdrop have been discovered growing here, including Galanthus nivalis 'Margery Fish' and Galanthus plicatus 'Lambrook Greensleeves'. Along with aconites, early cyclamen and crocuses, the snowdrops are planted in the famous ditch garden and in the woodland. A display bed showcases snowdrops that are available to buy in the nursery.
Visit www.eastlambrook.co.uk or call 01460 240328

Senior moments

At the end of my appointment, my GP told me about a new system for my prescription. It would now be sent online straight to my chemist. So she asked me which chemist I'm registered with. Without hesitation, I answered: "Lloyds, TSB." "I know the banks are diversifying," she laughed, "but I didn't realise they were dispensing tablets too."

R S Payne, Birmingham

Quick brain boost answer: **23** (the rule is +1,+2,+3 etc)

Recipe of the week

SCRAMBLED EGGS WITH SMOKED SALMON

Serves: 2
Preparation time:10 mins
Cooking time:15 mins

2 slices smoked salmon
4 tsp butter or margarine
4 eggs
400g (14oz) fresh spinach
500g (1lb2oz) new potatoes, peeled
Tbsp olive oil
Black pepper

1 Cut one slice of salmon into small pieces. Place into a small bowl and mix with the butter and black pepper to taste.
2 Halve the other slice of salmon.
3 Peel the potatoes and cook them for about 10 mins in boiling water until they are done.
4. Meanwhile, heat a large saucepan with a heavy bottom and pour in the oil. Beat the eggs, season with black pepper and pour them into the saucepan.
5 Cook over a low heat, stirring all the time, until almost set. Add half of the spinach and keep stirring until it has wilted. Remove the pan from the heat, stir in the salmon mixture and adjust the seasoning. Set aside and keep warm.
6 Quickly stir-fry the remaining spinach in a frying pan until wilted.
7 Place the halved salmon slices on 2 plates, spoon the scrambled eggs on top and serve immediately. Serve with the boiled potatoes and extra spinach on the side.
©www.flora.com

14 Monday

15 Tuesday

16 Wednesday

17 Thursday

18 Friday

19 Saturday

20 Sunday

Blast from the past

The scent of success

Barbara in her first two-piece.

I was working on the cosmetics counter in a department store in 1948 and we didn't sell all makes of perfumes as they were still in short supply, it being not long after the war. Eagle-eyed shoppers snapped up the more popular ones, such as Californian Poppy and Evening in Paris, as soon as they came in. My favourites were Coty's L'Aimant for evening occasions like dances and parties and for daytime I loved the lighter Gardenia, by Goya. Our mums liked Yardley Lavender and 4711 Eau de Cologne – also hard to get. In those days you dressed smartly for work and, even if the store was quiet, you were never allowed to be seen doing nothing. If there were no customers you made sure you had a duster in your hand so you could look busy at this never-ending chore!

In fact, Yardley were very kind to me. Their perfume, Bond Street, cost a guinea (as opposed to Californian Poppy at 2/3d). It was named after their famous store which opened in 1910 on New Bond Street and became a London landmark for a while. I knocked a bottle sideways, the top of one side broke off and there was no way I could stop it leaking. The smell of Yardley Bond Street was everywhere – gorgeous! I was mortified at my mistake. My manager suggested we write to them and explain, which we did. They sent us a new one, to much relief all round.

Barbara Bignell, Kettering, Northants

What a good idea!

When cooking a swede, I always find them so tricky to peel and chop as they're so hard. So now, before I get my peeler out, I always put the swede in the microwave for about ten minutes. The swede goes much softer after this, making it so much easier to work with and less of a strain on your hands.

Mrs M Vera, Croydon, Surrey

Garden inspiration

PIC: SHUTTERSTOCK

Jobs for March

◆ When bulbs have finished flowering, feed with organic fertiliser to encourage next year's blooms.
◆ Prune roses on a frost-free day.
◆ Rake lawns before cutting with the blades of the mower set high.
◆ Mulch round fruit trees and bushes to keep weed-free.
◆ Plant rhubarb crowns such as Timperley Early for forcing later in the season.
◆ Use old egg boxes to hold seed potatoes with the 'eye' end uppermost for chitting.
◆ Cut the canes of autumn-fruiting raspberries down to the ground.
◆ Wait until the end of the month to sow hardy annuals outside.

Senior moments

I needed some new lino for my bathroom so I went to my local DIY shop to try and find some. As I looked around, I just kept thinking how dull and drab all the colours looked, until one of the staff in the shop suggested that they might look much nicer if I took my sunglasses off.

Mrs T Pattison, Harrogate

Recipe of the week

CHOCOLATE STRAWBERRIES

Serves: 10
Preparation time: 30 mins
Cooking time: 10 mins

200g (7oz) dark chocolate
20 strawberries
100g (4oz) white chocolate buttons
Range of food colouring
Small cake decorations such as silver balls or hundreds and thousands

1 Start by melting the dark chocolate in a heatproof bowl over a pan of barely simmering water.
2 Once the chocolate has melted, remove from the heat, and allow to cool for 5 mins.
3. Holding the strawberry by the leaves dip it completely into the chocolate, right up to top.
4 Carefully lay the strawberry down on to the parchment paper and allow to cool completely. Continue with all the strawberries.
5 Melt the white chocolate in the same way. Once melted divide the chocolate into bowls and if using food colouring, colour the white chocolate with the different food colouring at this stage.
6 Drizzle the white chocolate over each strawberry using a teaspoon. Attach decorations while the white chocolate is still melted and tacky. Allow to set completely and serve.
©www.vivastrawberry.co.uk

21 Monday

22 Tuesday

23 Wednesday

24 Thursday

25 Friday

26 Saturday

27 Sunday

Blast from the past

My Italian adventure

Carole in her swimsuit in 1963.

My first trip abroad was in 1963, when I was 18 years old. I and three friends decided we'd like an adventure, so booked a holiday to Italy for 12 days with Arrowsmith tours – it cost us £34. We flew from Manchester to Ostend, then boarded a coach for 36 hours, stopping only for a bit of sightseeing, meals and toilets. We travelled through Belgium and Germany – where we saw storks building their nests on the chimney pots. In Switzerland we encountered strange toilets, just a square of tiles with a hole in the middle. You had to be careful to get out quickly or you got your feet wet when it flushed!

We had breakfast on day two overlooking Lake Como and passed through Milan – the beautiful cathedral looked like lace with all the figures on the outside. We arrived at our hotel at San Bartolomeo at 11.30pm. We were on the top floor with no lift! We had a glorious 12-day holiday and saw lots of things. Our hotel had its own beach and we went midnight swimming. One of my friends jumped into the sea and got little black things in her foot from a fish she jumped on and we spent until 3am with tweezers getting them out of her foot. We had a trip to Monte Carlo but weren't allowed in the casino as we were all under 21, and we travelled over the St Gotthard pass, which was very steep, windy and scary. I have never been abroad since but will always remember that holiday.

Carol Neville, Devon

What a good idea!

The cardboard tubes from the inside of kitchen rolls come in very handy so don't throw them away. Instead place them inside the leg of ladies' boots over spring and summer so that the leather doesn't wear away and lose its shape. This means when you dig out your boots again for winter they'll look as good as new.

Jenny Gildham, Cardiff

Quick brain boost

Can you unscramble this anagram to make an 11-letter word?

DEJA POD RISE

Answer below

Garden inspiration

PIC SHUTTERSTOCK

In bloom now: bronzy bergenias

All through the winter, bergenias provide interest with architectural leaves that are often tinged bronze or maroon. In early spring they reward us with clusters of bright red or pink flowers. Both the leaves and the flowers are favourites with flower arrangers as they look well in displays and last a long time once cut. Commonly known as Elephant's Ears, bergenias make excellent ground cover planted in groups under trees (they prefer partial shade). Bergenia 'Eric Smith' has rich red leaves that look striking when intermingled with dainty wood anemones.

Senior moments

I recently had a biopsy and was told to go to my GP in three weeks for the results. So I walked into my surgery three weeks later and asked the receptionist: "Have the results of my autopsy arrived yet?" It wasn't until she replied: "No, you're too early, love," that I realised what I'd said. Well, I am 82.

Gladys Stone, London

Quick brain boost answer: Jeopardised

Recipe of the week

SPECIAL DIPPY EGG & SOLDIERS

Serves: 1
Preparation time: 5 mins
Cooking time: 10 mins

1 large egg
4 spears of fresh green asparagus
2 slices of prosciutto ham
2 tbsp olive oil or coconut oil

1 Cut the slices of prosciutto in half width-ways.
2 Roll up the spears of asparagus in the prosciutto making sure they are tightly wrapped. Allow the spear end of the asparagus to remain unwrapped and visible.
3 Heat a non-stick frying pan and add the oil. Place the asparagus soldiers in the pan and cook over a medium heat. They need about 3-4 mins – roll them over every now and then.
4 To cook the egg, place in a small pan, cover with cold water, add a pinch of salt and place the pan on a high heat. When the water is almost boiling, gently stir the egg and boil for 3-4 mins.
5 Remove and serve as boiled eggs in an egg cup with the asparagus soldiers alongside.
©www.eggrecipes.co.uk

28 Monday

29 Tuesday

30 Wednesday

31 Thursday

1 Friday

2 Saturday

3 Sunday

Blast from the past

Enterprising Jill and Brian in their new school uniforms

Museum of childhood?

In the Easter school holiday, my friend Brian Kirby and I decided to make a museum in my dad's shed and 'open it to the public'. We were quite enterprising ten-year-olds having lived through the war years in London. We gathered our coin collections, stamp collections, Brownies and Cubs bits and pieces, etc. Then we went to nearby Barking Park (we lived in Ilford, Essex) and caught some 'tiddlers'. We then exhibited everything!

My mum, busy in the kitchen, became aware of all these children coming down the sideway into the garden towards the shed. When she came to investigate she was mortified to find we'd been charging a penny admission and promptly made us give back the pennies. I feel she and Brian's mum, who was a neighbour, must have had a good laugh though. The photo was taken in my garden that August, showing off our newly purchased school uniforms, having both passed the scholarship. The shed and summerhouse are in the background and we are standing on new grass, planted where the air raid shelter was and where my family slept underground on so many occasions over the war years.

Mrs Jill Edwards, Romford, Essex

What a good idea!

Has your plastic kettle turned black inside? There's no need to get a new kettle, you can easily clean it out. Just cut a lemon into slices and put these inside the kettle along with some fresh water. Bring the kettle to the boil and leave overnight. Then empty out the next day and your kettle should be shiny and clean.

Mavis Thomas, Birmingham

Quick brain boost

Garden inspiration

PIC: JOHN FIELDING

Visit Chiswick House Gardens

In March the Chiswick House Camellia Show invites visitors to admire its remarkable collection of camellias housed in the stunning 300-foot long conservatory. The plants include a rare example of Camellia 'Middlemist Red' (pictured) which, despite its name, has a deep pink bloom. The grounds surrounding the house are one of the earliest examples of an English landscaped garden designed by William Kent. A major restoration was completed four years ago and guided tours are recommended for anyone wishing to learn more of the garden's history.
Visit www.chgt.org.uk or call 0208 742 3905

Senior moments

A police car, all flashing lights and blaring siren made me pull my car over. A policeman then told me to step out of the car and turn around. Fully expecting to be handcuffed, I was surprised to see the officer pointing to the top of my car. It turned out that I'd been driving with my handbag on the roof.
Lorna White, Leeds

Quick brain boost answer: Incorrectly

Recipe of the week

SWEET POTATO & CHICKEN SKEWERS

Serves: 6
Preparation time: 10 mins
Cooking time: 15 mins

4 large skinless chicken breasts, cut into cubes
2 large sweet potatoes, peeled and cut into cubes
Fresh bay leaves
2 tbsp honey or sugar
6 skewers
For the marinade:
Juice of 2 oranges
1-2 chillies
5 sprigs of thyme
2 spring onions
Fresh ginger to taste
3 tbsp honey
Cracked black pepper

1 Cut the chillies, spring onions, thyme and ginger into thin strips and place into a large bowl.
2 Add the honey, orange juice, black pepper and mix well.
3 Add the chicken and gently mix together, marinating the chicken well. Cover and place in the fridge for at least one hour.
4 Cook the cubed sweet potatoes in boiling water for 4 mins, drain and set aside.
5 Cook the chicken on a griddle pan or on a BBQ until juices run clear, turning frequently. Drain and reserve the marinade when cooked
6 Build the skewers, alternating between chicken, sweet potato and bay leaves.
7 Pour the reserved marinade in a pan with honey or sugar, bring to the boil and turn the heat down to reduce the marinade to a thick syrup.
8 Coat the chicken with the marinade and serve with a salad on the side.
© Felice Tocchini 2014

4 Monday

5 Tuesday

6 Wednesday

7 Thursday

8 Friday

9 Saturday

10 Sunday

Blast from the past

Janet and her brothers

Home from the war

It was a bright, sunny day in April 1945. Flags were draped around the family bungalow, across the four houses next door and on to my grandma's bungalow in the cul-de-sac where we lived. My mum had gone to London the day before and I was waiting with my two grandmas and an auntie and uncle. I stood on the coal bunker at my grandma's house and looked across Holes Bay in Poole to see if I could see the steam train that was coming our way from London. Who was on the train? It was my dad! I hadn't seen him since 1939 when I was eight months old and he had been taken a prisoner of war at Dunkirk. He was in Poland, in Stalag XXA for five long years.

A small group of neighbours had collected outside my home, some of them waving flags, then suddenly a car appeared around the corner of the road. My mum got out, followed by a soldier dressed in khaki. He was very thin, had no teeth and was thinning on top. (He was 42 years old.) It was my dad. The neighbours clapped and my eldest brother cried and my dad was ushered into the house. My dad was home again! This precious photo was taken in 1943 of me and two of my three brothers. It was sent to my father in the prisoner of war camp. He brought the photo back with him.

Janet Griffin, Southampton

What a good idea!

My dog's food comes in a huge big bag, which can really come in handy once it's empty for lots of other uses. I find it's really useful for collecting my garden rubbish so that I don't have to keep going to and from the compost pile. The bag is very strong and you can use it time and time again.

Barbara Fescione, Worcestershire

Garden inspiration

PIC: SHUTTERSTOCK

Great garden tip

Traditionally, parsley is planted on Good Friday but it is important not to sow the seeds before the soil has warmed up. As parsley seeds have a hard casing, it's a good idea to put them in an old cup and pour very hot water over them. Strain, then mix them with dry sand before sowing in ground that has been treated with well-rotted compost. Keep well watered and wait for four to six weeks for germination to occur. For a second crop, repeat this process in the summer.

Senior moments

A group of us were discussing holidays and I mentioned a Marrakesh break I'd seen advertised in the newspaper. Everyone was impressed with the offer, but my friend Sandy looked horrified and said: "Oh no, I can't stand them on that awful TV ad, let alone go on holiday to see them." We were all at a loss for words, until it transpired she thought I'd said 'meerkat break'. **Brenda Barr, Leeds**

Quick brain boost answer: 65,536
(multiply the previous number by itself)

Recipe of the week

EASTER BUNNY CUPCAKES

Serves: 12
Preparation time: 40 mins
Cooking time: 20 mins

190g (6³/₄oz) self-raising flour
190g (6³/₄oz) caster sugar
190g (6³/₄oz) margarine or butter
200g (7oz) white chocolate bar
3 free range eggs
454g (1lb) pack ready-to-roll white icing
1 tbsp honey
To decorate:
Strawberry laces
Chocolate buttons

1 Preheat the oven to 180°C/350°F/Gas Mark 4.
2 If you have a food processor add the eggs, spread, caster sugar and flour and pulse until well blended. If not, beat the spread with the sugar, then beat in the eggs and whisk in the flour until smooth.
3 Line a cupcake tin with paper cases, fill ³/₄ each with some mixture. Bake for 18-20 mins, until risen and firm to the touch.
4 Allow to cool then cut off the risen dome, to make the cakes flat on top, cut this piece into half for the ears
5 Roll out the icing, cut out rounds and put on the cakes. Brush on a thin layer of honey, grate the chocolate, and sprinkle over the honey. Make two holes and put the cut tops in as ears. Cut shapes from the ready-to-roll icing for its teeth, chocolate buttons for eyes, laces for whiskers and half a button for its nose.
©www.aldi.co.uk

11 Monday

12 Tuesday

13 Wednesday

14 Thursday

15 Friday

16 Saturday

17 Sunday

Blast from the past

Joan, left, on The Strand with her friend

An exciting wartime day!

I was 24 years old. At 8.30 in the morning I stepped smartly out of Charing Cross station and made my way to the Hotel Metropole, where I worked as a clerical officer for the Ministry of Transport. The war had been going on for five years and so we had grown used to the gunfire and roaring planes so, although the siren had been sounded, I didn't go for cover but just went into the large ground-floor room where I worked. There was only one occupant, 'old' Mr Connell (he was 59!) I called out 'Good Morning', before I left my library book and knitting bag on my desk as I went out to the cloakroom in the next corridor. Only a few minutes passed before the whole building seemed to shudder as if we had been hit. I dashed round to rescue Mr Connell and found him staggering out of the door looking like a ghost – he was covered in plaster and had a beard like Father Christmas!

I went into the room to my desk – but looked in vain. Evidently the bomb exploded on its way down, having hit the building at an angle and took my desk with it through a hole in the floor. No excitement in those days. Half an hour later two elderly messengers appeared, harrumphed a bit, then said: "We'll have to move you up a bit." This happened and I was seated on a new floor at a desk which looked as if it had really been through the wars. Next came an in tray and out tray. So that was it. Somewhere to sit, somewhere to lean on and I was back in business!

Joan Ashton, Orpington, Kent

What a good idea!

The bristles on a paintbrush can easily get out of shape and become useless after a while, and proper paintbrushes aren't always cheap to replace. But if you put an old hair bobble around the bristles once you've cleaned and dried it, it will keep its shape and last for much longer. **Mrs J Gray, County Durham**

Quick brain boost

Garden inspiration

PIC: ALAMY

Jobs for April

◆ Sow seeds of herbaceous perennials in trays or
into the ground.
◆ Half-hardy annuals can be sown under a frame
to protect from frost.
◆ Apply fertiliser and selective weedkiller to lawns.
◆ Plant main crop potatoes in drills.
◆ Vegetable seeds, such as beetroot and carrots,
can be sown in the ground.
◆ On the rockery, divide early-flowering gentians
and saxifrages after flowering.
◆ In the pond, plant water lilies. Lift and divide
overgrown water lilies.
◆ Winter-flowering heathers can be lightly
trimmed back.
◆ Plant out sweet peas in a sunny position.
Support with canes.

Senior moments

I was going to bed and was just about to switch the
light off in our hallway. All of sudden my husband
called out to me to leave the light on. I said to him:
"Why? Is it a low calorie one?" I, of course, meant a
low-energy light, but at least it gave us both a good
laugh.   **Mrs Roberts, Northants**

Recipe of the week

SLOW-COOKED SHOULDER OF LAMB

Serves: 6
Preparation time: 30 minutes
Cooking time: 4-5 hours

1 boneless shoulder of lamb
1 head of garlic
$^1/_2$ bunch of rosemary
2 peeled carrots
50ml (2floz) olive oil
Salt and pepper
400g (14oz) whole round peeled shallots
20g ($^3/_4$oz) tomato purée
Pinch of flour
1 litre (1$^3/_4$pt) of chicken stock

1 Preheat oven to 160°C/325°F/Gas Mark 3.
  Remove any large fat deposits from the joint.
2 Stab the joint several times and insert one $^1/_2$ clove
  of garlic and a sprig of rosemary per incision.
3 Place the lamb on the 2 carrots cut just in half,
  drizzle over the olive oil and season.
4 Place in the oven for 4-5 hours, covering with a
  sheet of foil for the first 3 hours. With one hour to
  go, add the peeled shallots and remove the foil.
5 When the lamb is cooked, remove everything from
  the tray and allow to rest somewhere warm.
6 Add the tomato purée and flour to the cooking
  tray and place back on the stove to cook slightly.
  Then add the stock and bring to the boil.
7 Strain through a very fine sieve into a clean pan
  and bring back to the boil, season if required and
  serve.
© www.UKshallot.com

18 Monday

19 Tuesday

20 Wednesday

21 Thursday

22 Friday

23 Saturday

24 Sunday

Blast from the past

Vera in her school uniform

My happy schooldays

In 1922, aged five years old, I went to a private girls school called Belmont House in Clapham Park Road in South London. It was run by four sisters, and the teachers were Miss Maud, Miss Amy, Miss Jessy and Miss Betty. They were all very kind and there was never any shouting. The school was in a large house spread out over four floors. The playground was a very large garden, where we also played netball. I remember desks made of strong wood where we stored our books – no lockers with keys in those days. And while the teachers did keep a cane on their desks, I only ever remember it being used to point at the backboard with. Anyone that was naughty was stood in the corner – but I can never remember that happening. We were happy to be good – or do I just have rose-tinted glasses on?

There were no school dinners and lunch break was from 12 to 2pm to allow us to go home to eat. The schoolday finished at 4pm. At Christmas time we put on plays and our parents came to watch. Many of the girls had parties at Christmas and we would go to each other's houses in our party frocks where we would have the chance to show off our talents – be it playing the piano, singing or dancing. I left school at 12 years old and went to work at 14, but I look back with happiness on those times and the friends.

Vera Hilton, Weston Super Mare

What a good idea!

This is a great tip if you struggle to get your duvet in the cover. Just ruffle up the cover so that you can get the duvet into the top corners. Hold the duvet in place with two spring clothes pegs and give the duvet a shake. Then do the same with the bottom corners, securing this end with two other pegs.

Margaret McLester, Rutland

Quick brain boost

Garden inspiration

PIC: SHUTTERSTOCK

In bloom now: brilliant tulips

Some early tulips flower in March but April is the month when this much-prized bulb brings swathes of welcome colour to our parks and gardens. Single varieties such as 'Prinses Irene' and 'Couleur Cardinal' look splendid in pots as well as planted in beds amid a haze of blue forget-me-nots or blazing orange and yellow wallflowers. Flower arrangers use the red, green and gold parrot tulip 'Rococo' to make a flamboyant indoor display. And, an exception to the general rule, the orange-hued 'Ballerina' is sweetly scented, too.

Senior moments

I was recently at the supermarket, when the cashier asked me if I would like a voucher for a leg of lamb. I replied: "Yes, that would go down very nicely with some mint sauce, thank you." Seeing her strange look at me, I suddenly realised that she'd actually asked me if I'd like a voucher for Legoland!

Maureen Shears, Stirling

Quick brain boost answer: Exquisitely

Recipe of the week

PANCETTA & RED PEPPER BITES

Serves: 6
Preparation time: 15 mins
Cooking time: 20 mins

12 slices pancetta
1 medium onion, finely diced
1 red pepper, finely diced
6 eggs
50ml (2floz) milk
100g (4oz) cheddar, finely grated
Olive oil for frying
Salt and freshly ground black pepper

1 Preheat oven to 180°C/350°F/Gas Mark 4.
2 Heat a non-stick frying pan and fry the pancetta over a medium heat until crisp and brown. Remove from pan and drain on kitchen paper.
3 In the same pan, add a little olive oil if necessary and gently sweat down the onions and the peppers until soft but not coloured. Allow to cool a little.
4 Beat together the eggs, milk and 75g (3oz) of the cheese and season to taste.
5 Crumble the pancetta into smallish pieces and mix with the onions and red pepper. Divide this mixture between the muffins then top up each hole with some of the egg mixture, again dividing this equally. Top with a sprinkle of the remaining cheddar.
6 Place the muffin tin in the oven and cook for 18–20 mins until set and golden.

©www.facebook.com/EggsForSoldiers

25 Monday

26 Tuesday

27 Wednesday

28 Thursday

29 Friday

30 Saturday

1 Sunday

Blast from the past

Mary in her crêpe paper costume watched by her friends

Let's put on a show

I grew up in a close community in Shepperton, south-west of London and all the children played together, mostly outside in the road – not many cars back then. I was good friends with four other girls and we liked to act out plays. My mother often wrote them and we used the wooden garage at the side of our house as the stage with an old brown army blanket making do as our curtain. Our families did not have much money so our enterprising mothers made our costumes out of crêpe paper. We often roped in my younger brother to be a pixie or an elf. He had a beautiful suit made of brown velvet and learned to skip around the stage when he was needed! We charged our parents and the neighbours a penny to watch, which we posted off to Dr Barnardo's for children not so lucky as we were.

My older sister had been to dance lessons and tried her hardest to make a dancer out of me. I was tall, skinny and gawky at the best of times, but she tried very hard. This photo is of me, aged ten, in the garden posing in a position she had placed me in and my two best friends in the background were getting very bored with it all. The dress was pink crêpe paper and I was supposed to represent 'summer'. They were such happy, carefree times and we are all lucky enough to still be the best of friends.

Mary Archer, Middx

Quick brain boost

Can you solve this riddle?
If you have me, you want to share me but if you share me, you haven't got me. What am I?

Answer below

Garden inspiration

PIC: ALAMY

Great garden tip

Although moles are endearing creatures, the mounds of earth they create all over your lawn are not. Instead of killing them, discourage these unwelcome visitors by burying empty bottles in the vicinity of the molehills. Leave a few inches of the bottlenecks exposed above ground so that when the wind blows they will create a high-pitched singing sound that moles hate. Moles are also reputed to dislike the smell from certain spurges so it is worth planting Euphorbia lathyrus and Euphorbia lactea if they continue to be a nuisance.

Senior moments

I was looking after my granddaughter the other day, when she asked me, very sweetly, whether I would ever like to be famous. Without a moment's hesitation, I replied: "No, I don't think I would. Not if it meant being followed around all day by the Pavarotti." I, of course, meant the paparazzi. What a thought! **June Layton, East Sussex**

What a good idea!

Even if your old anorak or coat is too worn down to wear outside as normal, it can still come in useful. If you cut off the sleeves, you can wear them as arm protectors for when you're pruning prickly plants and shrubs. You can keep the sleeves in place just with a wide hair band or by safety pinning them to your blouse. **Pamela Johnson, Wakefield**

Quick brain boost answer: A secret

Recipe of the week

ASPARAGUS TART

Serves: 8
Preparation time: 10 mins
Cooking time: $1^{1}/_{4}$ hours

60g ($2^{1}/_{2}$oz) butter
2 tbsp olive or rapeseed oil
750g (1lb 11oz) red onions, peeled and thinly sliced
3 sprigs fresh thyme
1 sprig rosemary
1 bay leaf
2 tsp soft light brown sugar
1 packet ready-rolled puff pastry
2 bundles asparagus
1 egg, beaten

1. Preheat the oven to 200°C/400°F/Gas Mark 6.
2. Melt the butter with the oil in a saucepan. Add the onions cook on a gentle heat, stirring from time to time, until soft.
3. Add the herbs and sugar, increase the heat and cook until the onions are caramelised. Leave to cool, discarding the herb sprigs and bay leaf.
4. Place the ready-rolled puff pastry sheet on a greased baking sheet. Score a 2cm ($^{3}/_{4}$in) deep border around the outside of the pastry, making sure you don't cut all the way through.
5. Trim and halve the asparagus. Pile the caramelised onions into the centre of the tart and spread out to the inner edge of the border.
6. Place the asparagus on top, season and drizzle with olive oil. Brush the border with the beaten egg and bake in the pre-heated oven for 20 mins until golden brown. Reduce the oven to 180°C/350°F/Gas Mark 4 and bake for a further 20 mins.

©www.british-asparagus.co.uk

2   Monday

3   Tuesday

4   Wednesday

5   Thursday

6   Friday

7   Saturday

8   Sunday

Blast from the past

A day trip to Holland was an ambitious outing in the Sixties

Day trip to Holland

As a young wife and mum in the late Sixties I had never been abroad, although I lived almost next door to what is now Newcastle International Airport. I was a secretary to a local Young Wives' group and about to organise an outing, so I was delighted to see an advert for a day trip to Keukenhof Park in Holland. The response from the group was overwhelming, and very soon I had over 40 names for this very ambitious day out. Like me, it was a first for many of the members and we all scrambled to get our first passports. At that time it was simpler to get a yearly passport. Lots of grans had to be involved too, for childminding.

There was great excitement and nerves tingling on our arrival at the airport on the morning of the outing. Then panic! One of the group who had worked and lived abroad had forgotten her passport. Fortunately, there was time for her to nip home to retrieve it. Our cameras clicked on the lovely gardens, on the canals and on the windmills and the sun certainly had its hat on for us. We arrived home full of chatter and amazed to see so many husbands and children meeting us off the plane. How times have changed – I'm still in touch with many of those young wives, most of whom are now well travelled, but we still talk about that lovely day out and the fun we shared.

Pat Berkshire, Northumberland

What a good idea!

It's easy to make a waterproof kneeler to use when you're out in the garden, weeding and putting plants in. Just place an old cushion pad you have inside a supermarket Bag for Life. Seal this with some sellotape and then you're good to go, even if the ground in your garden is still wet from rain showers.

Mrs A Young, Cheshire

Garden inspiration

Visit Myddelton House

Myddelton House in Enfield was the home of dedicated plant collector E A Bowles who was known as The Crocus King. After his death in 1954 the garden he created fell into disrepair but is now being restored to its former glory. Many of Bowles' original plants remain in the grounds, including ones that were named after him such as the wallflower Erysimum Bowles's Mauve. Home to a national collection of irises, the gardens also have a restored Victorian kitchen garden and conservatory. **Visit info@leevalleypark.org.uk or call 08456 770 600**

Senior moments

I'd just had a shower and had put my dirty socks from the day into the washing machine. Or so I thought. It was only later when I went to get the milk out of the fridge to make a tea that I spotted that I'd, in fact, left my socks in the fridge rather than the washing machine. Well they are both white!

Barbara Newson, by email

Recipe of the week

CHEESE, CELERY & WALNUT SCONES

Makes:15
Preparation time: 20 mins
Cooking time: 10-12 mins

225g (8oz) self-raising flour
2 tsp baking powder
50g (2oz) butter
125g (4¹/₂oz) mature cheddar cheese, grated
1 head celery, finely chop 2 of the stalks
50g (2oz) walnuts, roughly chopped
1 large free-range egg
6 tbsp milk

1 Preheat oven 220°C/425°F/Gas Mark 7 and grease a baking tray.
2 Place the flour and baking powder into a large bowl, rub in the butter until it resembles fine breadcrumbs and then stir in the celery, 100g (4oz) of the grated cheese and the chopped walnuts.
3 Break the egg into a measuring jug, lightly beat and make up to 150ml with the milk, add all but a small amount, reserve to brush the tops with. Mix gently until you have a soft dough.
4 Knead lightly on a floured surface and roll out to approx. 2cm (³/₄in) thick, cut into 6cm (2¹/₂in) rounds and place on the baking tray.
5 Brush the tops with a little of the reserved egg mix and sprinkle with the remaining cheese, bake for 12-15 mins until well risen and golden. Cool on a wire rack.
©www.fenlandcelery.com

9 Monday

10 Tuesday

11 Wednesday

12 Thursday

13 Friday

14 Saturday

15 Sunday

Blast from the past

Jill and her dad heading to school on their tandem

Early lessons in life

Dad was always smiling and made sure we enjoyed the outdoor life. When I was about eight years old we had a tandem, which was later fitted with a 'Power Pak' petrol engine and sometimes I'd get taken to school on the back. Despite him owning a cycle shop, I was 12 or 13 before I acquired my first bike. He made sure I'd done plenty of extra chores to earn the privilege. Oh boy, was I proud of that bike! It had a three-speed, a dynamo and skirt guard, but best of all a tennis racquet-cum-hockey stick holder on the front forks.

In 1956, when I was 11, and long before foreign holidays were the norm, my mum and dad took me on a Mediterranean cruise on the SS Orcades. Mum made me a red-gored skirt with matching fitted jacket with scalloped edging especially for the occasion – I can still picture it. I was in awe of all I saw – especially the foreign tongues, smells and unknown way of life away from home. On shore in the back streets, shoeless children would pick up the hems of our skirts and feel the material between their fingers and beg for coins. The contrast left a lasting impression on me and I still appreciate what I have to this day. Thanks, Mum and Dad for those early lessons in what is really important.

Jill Goodesmith, Bristol

What a good idea!

I always find the worse bit of cutting my hedge to be clearing away the rubbish at the end. So to save yourself time, lay a ground sheet or even an old bed sheet on the ground around the hedge before you begin. Then when you're done, you can just gather the sheet ends in and empty the leaves straight into the bin. **Mrs M Dinsdale, Northumberland**

Quick brain boost

Recipe of the week

Garden inspiration

Jobs for May

◆ Prune early-flowering shrubs such as Kerria japonica and Prunus triloba.

◆ Start spraying roses against pests and diseases. Apply a general rose fertiliser.

◆ Once the danger of frost is over, plant out dahlias and half-hardy annuals.

◆ Thin out seedlings of vegetables planted in April.

◆ Sow half-hardy vegetables such as runner beans and courgettes.

◆ Lift tulip bulbs after flowering to make room for summer bedding plants.

◆ Sow biennials such as foxgloves and Canterbury bells.

◆ Avoid the crowds and enjoy the TV coverage of the Chelsea Flower Show from the comfort of your armchair!

GRILLED VEGETABLE FLATBREADS

Serves: 2
Preparation time: 15 mins
Cooking time: 10 mins

1 courgette (or $^1/_2$ courgette and $^1/_2$ aubergine)
1 yellow pepper
125g (4$^1/_2$oz) cherry tomatoes
$^1/_2$ tbsp olive oil
1 small bunch mixed fresh herbs (e.g. dill, chives or parsley)
4 tsp butter or margarine
5 tbsp tinned kidney beans, rinsed and drained
3 sundried tomatoes
1 spring onion
1 large flatbread
Black pepper

1 Preheat the grill.
2 Slice the courgette. Deseed the pepper and slice into pieces. Halve the cherry tomatoes.
3 Brush the vegetables lightly with the olive oil and grill for a few minutes until golden brown. Turn every now and then. Sprinkle with black pepper.
4 Roughly chop the herbs. Rinse and drain the kidney beans. Soak the sundried tomatoes in water.
5 Using a hand blender, whizz together the butter, kidney beans, sundried tomatoes and spring onion. Add half the herbs and black pepper to taste. Divide the flatbread and place on two plates. Spread with the tomato and bean topping. Arrange the grilled vegetables on top. Sprinkle over the remaining herbs and black pepper. Fold over and serve immediately.

©www.flora.com

Senior moments

I was in Argos when I needed my reading glasses, so I started fumbling about in my handbag to find them. A young shop assistant noticed me looking a bit stressed and asked if she could help. When I explained to her that I was all right, I was just looking for my glasses, she smiled as she pointed out: "But you are wearing them."

Lilian Smith, Preston

16 Monday

17 Tuesday

18 Wednesday

19 Thursday

20 Friday

21 Saturday

22 Sunday

Blast from the past

Those wonderful Whit walks

A big part of my childhood in Bury in Lancashire was taking party in the Whit Friday Walks. It was a day that the whole town celebrated. The shops would close and the roads would be blocked off and the streets would fill with spectators from around 8.30am. The catholic churches had their walk on Whit Sunday and the other churches on Friday. Each walk was led by two men carrying a banner, then a young girl was chosen as Queen for the year with her court of attendants, all beautifully dressed. The rest of the congregation would walk behind them. With many churches in the town you can imagine how packed the town centre would be with families and friends. After we had walked around the main streets, we would gather on the market square for a short service and then return to our own churches. Once home, we would take off our new clothes and then spend the afternoon in a nearby park playing games and enjoying a picnic. Each church hired a brass band for the morning to lead us around the town – that for me was the best part as I just loved walking behind them and hearing the wonderful music they played. I can still remember the burst of pride and excitement I felt when they struck the first note and we left the church to begin the walk.

Mrs J Slocombe, Essex

What a good idea!

Don't throw away your old eggshells. Instead, give them a wash and leave them to dry in a tub on the windowsill. Then once they're completely dry, crush them into a fine grit and scatter this between the vegetables and flowers in your garden. Pests hate all the jagged edges and so are likely to leave your best garden crops alone. **Babs Handling, South Ayrshire**

Quick brain boost

Garden inspiration

In bloom now: exquisite blossom

May, as the Andrews Sisters' song goes, is apple-
blossom time. And it's the month when plum, pear
and cherry trees also cover their branches with
a delicate froth of pink or white flowers which,
seen against the backdrop of a clear blue sky, has
inspired poets and songwriters down the ages. In
the country, orchards buzz with bees and other
pollinating insects, while city dwellers stroll
beneath the canopy of cherry trees that line the
streets and scatter the pavements with pastel
petals. Summer is just around the corner!

Senior moments

I thought I would try out a perfume sample I had
received by spraying a little behind my ear. I then
looked in the mirror to start putting on my make-up
when I saw two cream streaks trickling down my
neck. I then realised that I had sprayed a sample of
eye serum behind each ear rather than perfume.

Alison Lane, by email

Quick brain boost answer: Chimpanzees

Recipe of the week

LEMON DRIZZLE CAKE

Serves: 8–10
Preparation time: 15 mins
Cooking time: 35 mins

175g (6oz) unsalted butter
175g (6oz) caster sugar
Grated zest and juice of 2 lemons
Greek–style natural low–fat yogurt
2 large eggs, beaten
175g (6oz) self-raising flour
3 tbsp caster sugar
150g (5oz) icing sugar, sifted
$^1/_2$ tbsp water

1 Preheat the oven to 180°C/350°F/Gas Mark 4.
  Grease and line a round 15cm (6in) loose bottom
  cake tin.
2 Cream together the butter and sugar in a bowl.
3 Add the grated zest of lemons and yogurt then
  add the eggs.
4 Add the flour, mix well and spoon the mixture into
  the prepared tin, ensure a level surface.
5 Bake in the oven for 35 mins or until a skewer
  comes out clean.
6 Transfer to a cooling rack.
7 In a small saucepan add the juice of the
  lemons with the remaining 3 tbsp of sugar
  and allow to reduce on a high heat. Leave to
  cool slightly.
8 Using a skewer prick the cake all over and then
  pour the lemon sugar syrup all over the top, allow
  it to soak in. Leave to cool completely before icing
9 Mix the icing sugar with the water until a runny
  paste consistency is achieved. Using a spoon
  drizzle the icing liberally backwards and forwards
  over the cake.

©www.rachelsorganic.co.uk

23 Monday

24 Tuesday

25 Wednesday

26 Thursday

27 Friday

28 Saturday

29 Sunday

Blast from the past

Newlyweds Adrian and Margaret Dickinson

Married in May

I have wonderful memories of Whitsun in 1956 as on May 19 I was married to the most wonderful man (and still am). After the service in St Francis Xavier in Liverpool and after all the photos had been taken (which cost ten guineas and included an album and 24 slides) we went to Reeces in the city centre for the reception. The material for my dress was embossed with lily of the valley and I also had the same flowers in my bouquet. It wasn't a big wedding – I think there were about 35 guests and the meal cost 7/6d a head. The cake was about £2. We did not have an evening do as that wasn't the style then. For our honeymoon we went first to London and on the Sunday we went to Mass at Westminster Cathedral. On the Monday we left London and went to the Isle of Wight for me to meet Adrian's older sister who was and still is a Benedictine Nun in Ryde. It was a wonderful time.

We have been very blessed with our family, having one daughter and three sons, ten grandchildren and eight great-granddaughters, who have given us so much pleasure and happiness. God willing we will be celebrating our Diamond Wedding anniversary in 2016.

Margaret Dickinson, Liverpool

What a good idea!

It can be a real nuisance if ants keep getting into your house. But you can easily stop them coming in just by using a common kitchen ingredient. First, find out where the ants are getting in and then place some bay leaves around the entrance. Very soon your hoard of ants should disappear.

Clive Harris, Plymouth

Quick brain boost

Garden inspiration

PIC ALAMY

Great garden tip

This is the month to plant runner beans when the risk of frost is over. These are thirsty plants that do best in cool, moist conditions. A traditional and cost-effective trick to retain water in the soil is to put sheets of newspaper in the newly dug trenches along with plenty of well-rotted compost, leaf mould and manure. The absorbent newspaper retains moisture for a long time even during dry spells. Remember to water runner beans regularly and mulch if there is any danger of drought.

Senior moments

I have recently had both of my hip joints replaced, although I find that one of them is almost always cold and numb. Anyway, one day when I was in the car with my daughter, I kept rubbing my hip saying: "I just have no feeling." She fell about laughing. "I'm not surprised, Mum," she said, "you're rubbing the edge of the car seat."   **Susan Fermor, Reading**

Quick brain boost answer: His breath

Recipe of the week

STICKY CHILLI PRAWNS

Serves: 4
Preparation time: 8 mins
Cooking time: 10 mins

1 tbsp Flora Cuisine
1 large onion, diced
1 large red pepper, diced
1 large clove garlic, crushed
2½cm (1in) piece fresh root ginger, grated
400g (14oz) raw peeled prawns (thawed if frozen)
4 tbsp tomato ketchup
Tabasco sauce, to taste
2 tbsp fresh coriander, chopped
Squeeze of lemon juice

1 Heat the Flora Cuisine in a frying pan. Add in the onion and fry until softened. Add red pepper and fry, stirring for 2-3 mins.
2 Add in garlic and ginger and fry for a further 2-3 mins.
3 Add the prawns and fry, stirring, until they have just turned pink.
4 Add tomato ketchup and Tabasco sauce to taste.
5 Add coriander and a squeeze of lemon juice.
6 Cook for 2-3 mins, until the prawns are cooked and the sauce is sticky. Serve with either toasted pitta bread or rice.
© www.flora.com

30	Monday

31	Tuesday

1	Wednesday

2	Thursday

3	Friday

4	Saturday

5	Sunday

Blast from the past

Barbara (right) and Valerie at Windsor Castle

Bike ride to Windsor

When my friend Valerie and I were old enough to ride our bikes on the main roads, my mum would take us out for a picnic. One route from Hillingdon in Middlesex where we lived, was the 12 or so leg-aching miles to Windsor Castle. We forgot the strenuous part at the thought of the picnic, not to mention seeing this famous castle and especially Queen Mary's Dolls' House (we weren't as old as we looked in the photo – just tall and wearing our school blazers).

In the Forties, you could stop at a farmer's field, go through the gate if there was one, spread out your mac' (no car blanket then) and get out the picnic goodies – although at that time we didn't call them that! When my mum was working, Valerie's parents would let me take my ready-prepared dinner round to them (they lived at next-door-but-one) and eat with their family. Then sometimes we'd go for a walk in the field and woods near our homes. We are certainly very lucky, as we are still best friends and now in our 80s. Mind you, we live some 90 miles or more apart now, so popping round for lunch is not so easy!

Barbara Bignell, Northants

What a good idea!

Stop bananas over-ripening too fast by keeping them in the fridge, especially in summer or if your fruit bowl is in a very warm area. You'll find the banana skin does start to get a lot darker when it's in the fridge, but the fruit inside will stay firm and fresh for much longer.

Barbara Child, Cornwall

Quick brain boost

What comes next in this number sequence?

17, 34, 68, 136, 272, ???   Answer below

Garden inspiration

PIC: PICTON CASTLE TRUST

Visit Picton Castle Gardens

Late spring is the ideal time to see the magnificent rhododendrons for which Picton Castle in Pembrokeshire is famed. Don't miss 'Old Port' which was planted in 1860 and has claims to be the biggest rhododendron in the world. Unique to Picton is the hybrid R 'Salmon Jubilee' bred by former head gardener, Leo Ekkes. Other attractions include a 'jungle garden' of exotic plants and a walled garden where the dramatic spires of Echium pininana emerge towards the end of May.

**Visit www.pictoncastle.co.uk
or call 01437 751326**

Senior moments

When my mum answered the phone the other day, the lady at the other end said: "I am ringing about your husband's eye screening." My mum told her to please wait and straight away shouted up the stairs to my dad: "Rory, have you ordered some ice cream?" Needless to say, everyone was a bit confused, especially my dad.

Mrs J Deakin, Sheffield

Quick brain boost answer: **544** (the rule is x 2)

Recipe of the week

VANILLA, STRAWBERRY & ROSE CAKE

Serves: 12
Preparation time: 30 mins
Cooking time: 30 mins

For the cake:
175g (6oz) self-raising flour
1/2 level tsp baking powder
175g (6oz) Stork tub margarine
175g (6oz) caster sugar
3 medium eggs
1 tsp vanilla extract
For the filling:
115g (4oz) icing sugar
40g (1 1/2 oz) Stork margarine
1-2 tsp rosewater
150g (5oz) strawberries, sliced
55g (2oz) icing sugar for glacé icing
A little pink food colouring

1 Sift the flour and baking powder into a large mixing bowl, add the remaining cake ingredients and beat with a wooden spoon until smooth.
2 Spoon the mixture into 2 greased and base lined 20cm (8in) cake tins.
3 Bake in a preheated oven at 180°C/350°F/Gas Mark 4 for 30-40 mins or until cooked. Turn out on to a wire tray.
4 Place the icing sugar, margarine and rosewater in a bowl and mix well until smooth. Spread the base cake with the icing and three-quarters of the strawberries. Top with the second cake.
5 Decorate with a thin glacé icing made with the icing sugar and a little water or rosewater and a few drops of pink food colouring. Drizzle over the top of the cake. Finish with edible flowers.
©www.bakewithstork.com

6 Monday

7 Tuesday

8 Wednesday

9 Thursday

10 Friday

11 Saturday

12 Sunday

Blast from the past

Days out were enjoyed to a variety of destinations

Days out with the Buffaloes

My late father was a member of the Buffaloes in Fifties Portsmouth. It was a secret society for men, similar to the Freemasons, that did a lot of charity work. Dad attended the meetings each week and had a secret password to gain entry. Happily for us, families were invited to the many social events including Christmas parties and summer outings. A coach took us to various places including the New Forest, Stonehenge and Bournemouth. On the way we stopped off at a few cafés and pubs for refreshment and at our destination there would often be a light lunch provided for us. I remember at one, a long table was laid out with a plated ham salad for each person, with jelly and fruit to finish, then bread and jam and pots of tea. After this we children were free to explore the area and have a run around.

On the way home there were crates of beer and lemonade on board and a few more comfort stops as too much drink may have been consumed during the day. There was always a sing-along until eventually most people, me included, fell asleep due to the motion of the coach.

Valerie Reilly, Reading

What a good idea!

If you are eating outside in the summer weather, it's easy to run out of room on your table and chairs for everything you need. But you can get some extra space for your cutlery and crockery and anything you want by opening up a small step ladder. It makes an ideal set of shelves and takes up very little room.

Anne Darby, Burndon

Quick brain boost

Garden inspiration

Jobs for June

◆ Continue spraying roses.
◆ Cut down early flowering perennials to three inches above ground.
◆ Plant De Caen anemones to flower in the autumn.
◆ Keep on top of the weeding by hoeing, especially in the vegetable garden.
◆ Once any danger of frost is over, plant out tomatoes, sweet corn and peppers.
◆ Harvest early potatoes and early salad crops.
◆ Prune evergreen shrubs so that new growth has time to harden up before winter.
◆ Prune early-flowering clematis such as C montana and C alpina.
◆ Deadhead lilacs, rhododendrons and azaleas after they have flowered.

Senior moments

I came in from the garden as my daughters were talking and I heard the word 'tablet' being mentioned. So I went over to my medicine drawer and said: "I have Ibuprofen and Paracetamol. Please do help yourself to what you need." They both laughed. "Oh no, Mum" they said, "we were talking about a type of computer tablet".

Susan Snell, West Sussex

Recipe of the week

STRAWBERRY HONEYCOMB SUNDAE

Serves: 4
Preparation time: 10 mins
Cooking time: n/a

400g (14oz) strawberries
1 tsp icing sugar
150ml (¼ pt) double cream
1 vanilla pod
1 tbsp of runny honey
100ml (4floz) low-fat Greek yogurt
300g (10½oz) raspberries
300g (10½oz) of honeycomb, broken up

1 Hull and half the strawberries then mix with the icing sugar. Place on one side and let them marinate while you prepare the cream.
2 Pour the cream into a bowl and add the vanilla seeds scraped from the pod and the honey. Whip the cream to form soft peaks and then fold in the Greek yogurt.
3 Take four little glass bowls and divide the strawberry mix between each one, then pile on some vanilla honey cream.
4 Next, add a layer of raspberries and cover with some more vanilla honey cream. Finally, sprinkle the honeycomb on top of the cream and top with a whole strawberry cut in half.

©www.sweetevestrawberry.co.uk

13 Monday

14 Tuesday

15 Wednesday

16 Thursday

17 Friday

18 Saturday

19 Sunday

Blast from the past

Enjoying the delights of Barbados

Going to Barbados

I didn't have my first foreign holiday until I was 40. With four children we had always had camping holidays in the UK but my husband was serving with the Royal Navy and he had been to South Georgia and the Falklands for six long months. As a treat, at the end of the deployment the Navy spent one week in Barbados and allowed the wives and girlfriends to join their men (we had to pay). I was terrified, especially as I didn't know anyone who was going, but it was the chance of a lifetime so I said yes. I ran a Cub Pack at the time so two of the leaders offered to look after our children and between church friends and scouting friends I managed. I met the other women at Heathrow – I was terrified of flying and the take off was awful but once we were up I was fine and coped well. I had a wonderful time, I remember eating flying fish and enjoying the laid-back atmosphere. I had to visit a doctor while I was there and when he called me in asked me if I knew who I had been chatting to in the waiting room. When I said no, he replied: "That was Scobie Breasley the retired English jockey." I hadn't heard of him but, of course, when I checked with Peter's mum and my dad they were impressed. Barbados gave me a taste for travel and since then I've been to almost every country in the world.

Lorraine Thompson, Staffs

What a good idea!

Fed up of seeing dust gather so quickly around your house? Dampen a soft cloth or duster in a little white vinegar and then wipe all the hard surfaces around your house with this. The white vinegar is great at stopping dust settling, meaning you won't have to go round dusting quite so often.

Jane Best, Nottingham

Garden inspiration

In bloom now: romantic roses

Tumbling over trellis arches, fanned against a brick wall or scrambling through a tree, climbing roses are the pride of an English garden. Unlike ramblers, they are repeat flowering so you can enjoy the perfect form and sweet perfume of a climber such as Compassion from June right through to December. If you love their beauty but object to being scratched by their thorns, the old favourite deep-pink Zepherine Drouhin is the rose for you. Where space is limited, patio roses such as Nice Day or Laura Ford can be grown in a container.

Senior moments

The other day my 89-year-old mum turned to me and said: "Would you like a cartwheel?" I was a bit surprised but I'd never seen her do one, so I said: "Yes please, have you got enough room in here?" We looked at each other a moment and then at the liquorice Catherine Wheels she was holding and the penny finally dropped.

Mrs S Gill, Exeter

Recipe of the week

ELDERFLOWER & GOOSEBERRY JELLY

Serves: 4-6
Preparation time: 15 mins
Setting time: 4 hours

2 x 300g (10^1/$_2$oz) tins of gooseberries in syrup
200ml (8floz) Belvoir Elderflower Cordial
200ml (8floz) water
12g (^{1}/$_2$oz) of sheet gelatine (7 sheets approx measuring 7^1/$_2$x11cm)
Fine kitchen muslin
1-1^1/$_2$pt jelly mould

1 Pour the cordial into a saucepan followed by the water and the gooseberries with their syrup.
2 Gently burst the berries with a potato masher. Bring the mixture to simmer.
3 In a separate bowl snap the gelatine into shards and cover in only just enough warm water to soak. The water must not be boiling, as it will destroy the properties of the gelatine. Leave it there until softened.
5 Pour the contents of the saucepan slowly into a muslin-lined sieve.
6 While the jelly syrup is still warm drop in the gelatine, pulling it apart as you add it, to eradicate lumps
7 Whisk until all the gelatine has totally dissolved, then pour straight into the mould and cover the top with cling film. Allow the jelly to set in the fridge for at least 4 hours
8 When ready to serve turn out the jelly on to a serving plate.
© www.belvoirfruitfarms.co.uk

June 20 - 26

20 Monday

21 Tuesday

22 Wednesday

23 Thursday

24 Friday

25 Saturday

26 Sunday

Blast from the past

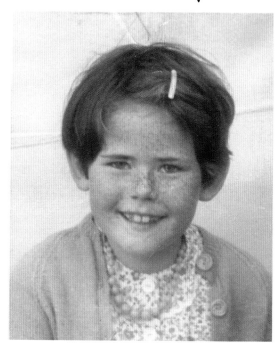

Jean's childhood home was alongside York racecourse

Days of chicks and horses

When I was young I lived near York racecourse. We had a large garden from which we could slip under the fence and be on the racecourse. We kept chickens in the garden and one of my jobs was to collect the eggs. I disliked this as the hens could be broody and, as such, would peck furiously if anyone tried to take their eggs. My answer was to take the family dog with me – he would put his head in the nest box and the hens would run, protesting as they went. Eggs collected, mission accomplished!

Our playground was the racecourse itself and in the hot summer months my friends and I would don our swimming costumes and play in the water sprinklers that were keeping the course in good condition – that is until the course officials shooed us away! We played circuses on the starting boxes, pretending they were high-wire apparatus. I can still remember the thrill of watching the start of a race, the sights, smells and anticipation of horse and rider as the starter dropped his flag and the horses set off. No stalls in those days. When the race meeting was over we would go to where the bookmakers' stands were and hunt for any coins that had been dropped by the punters. Sometimes we made a few pounds in halfcrowns and other coins. All such happy, uncomplicated days!

Jean Fisher, Leeds

Quick brain boost

Can you solve this riddle?

What occurs once in every minute, twice in every moment, yet never in a thousand years?

Answer below

Garden inspiration

PIC: SHUTTERSTOCK

Great garden tip

Don't throw away banana skins. They are rich in all the trace elements (magnesium, sulphur, calcium, silica and sodium) needed for roses to flourish. Every month through the growing season, place the skins just beneath the soil around the base of rose bushes. Or cut the skins into half-inch pieces, place in a glass quart jar and cover with water. Leave in a cool dark place for two weeks then purée the resulting sludge in a blender. Pour one cup of this into the ground around each rose bush.

Senior moments

I had to make a phone call to a council department, and told the person at the other end that I was calling on my husband's behalf. They transferred me to somebody else and when I was asked: "Who is calling?" I straight away replied: "I am my husband's wife." Well, we all ended up in fits of laughter.

Pam Edmunds, no address supplied

What a good idea!

It's always a nuisance when my potatoes start sprouting after just a few days of being left in the cupboard and have to be thrown out. But if you store them alongside a bag of apples, you'll find that they don't sprout quite as quickly and so they keep for a lot longer. **Mrs A Stock, Essex**

Quick brain boost answer: The letter **M**

Recipe of the week

CHICKEN, BACON & BEETROOT SALAD

Serves: 4
Preparation time: 10 mins
Cooking time: 10 mins

500g (1lb2oz) new potatoes, thickly sliced
Salad dressing of your choice
300g (10$^1/_2$ oz) long-stem broccoli, cut into 3-4cm (1$^1/_2$in-1$^3/_4$in) pieces
2 large chicken breasts, skinless and boneless
1 tbsp olive oil
8 slices smoked streaky bacon
2x200g (7oz) beetroot, cut into wedges
80g (3oz) bag baby salad leaves
80g(3oz) bag rocket

1 Bring a large pan of lightly salted water to the boil and add the potatoes. Cook for 10-15 mins until tender when pierced with the tip of a knife.
2 When the potatoes are nearly ready, add the broccoli and cook for a further 2 mins. Drain well and coat with salad dressing while still hot, tossing to mix.
3 Meanwhile, heat the oil in a frying pan until hot. Flatten the chicken breasts a little and season with a little salt and pepper, then fry for about 4-5 mins on each side until cooked through.
4 Remove, set aside to cool a little then slice on the diagonal. Add the bacon to the frying pan and fry until crisp. Roughly chop. Add the chicken and bacon to the bowl and toss together.
5 Finally, add the beetroot and leaves and lightly toss with a little more dressing and serve immediately.

©www.lovebeetroot.co.uk

27 Monday

28 Tuesday

29 Wednesday

30 Thursday

1 Friday

2 Saturday

3 Sunday

Blast from the past

Colette with her granny

An Irish childhood

I grew up in Northern Ireland, the eldest of ten children; there were six girls and four boys. As our family grew it was decided that I would be farmed out and go and live with our Granny, who lived opposite us. I was always very close to my Granny and spent a lot of time with her every day, so I didn't mind moving in with them. It meant I could have a bedroom all to myself. Granny also allowed me to used one drawer in her sideboard and I kept all my pencils and paper and paints in it. I loved having this wee drawer all to myself and I kept it very neat and tidy.

Granny's front door led into a very tiny hall with two doors off it. One opened into the living room and the other door led down into the dark and dingy cellar. I never relished the idea of going down those steep wooden steps. I had no option though, as the outdoor toilet was through the cellar and into a tiny outside yard. Next to the toilet was what was called the 'pit' where all the rubbish was put until the workmen came round to clean it out. Sometimes, when I went down to use the toilet, there would be a horrible rat in the trap just outside the toilet door. As you can imagine, I didn't spend too much time there! Times were hard but everyone managed to keep smiling.

Colette Turner, N Ireland

Quick brain boost

What comes next in this number sequence?

3, 20, 37, 54, 71, ??

Answer below

Garden inspiration

PIC: ROYAL NATIONAL ROSE SOCIETY

Visit The Gardens of the Rose

Roses are at their gorgeous best from June onwards and 1,800 old and new varieties can be admired in The Gardens of the Rose near St Albans in Hertfordshire. Under the auspices of The Royal National Rose Society, the gardens were revamped in 2006 and feature ornamental fish ponds as well as a stunning pergola of 72 arches. All the roses are labelled so this is the place to go to find which is the right rose for your garden.

Visit www.rnrs.org.uk or call 0845 833 4344

Senior moments

I'd just bought two new bras at Marks & Spencer, along with two boxes of frozen fish and had put all my shopping away at home. I then decided I'd go and try on the bras I'd bought, but I couldn't find them anywhere. After a long search, I finally tracked them down. They were, of course, in the freezer with the fish.   **Maureen Barron, Llandudno**

What a good idea!

To help keep myself cool on hot summer nights, I fill up my hot-water bottle with ice-cold water from the tap. Throughout the night, I move the bottle around my bed or keep my feet on it to cool me right down. It's a great way of making sure I get a good night's sleep.

Rhoda Pippen, Cardiff

Quick brain boost answer: 88 (the rule is +17)

Recipe of the week

STRAWBERRY SOUFFLÉS

Serves: 4
Preparation time: 10 mins
Cooking time: 15 mins

1 tbsp butter
4 large free-range egg whites
125 g (4oz) caster sugar
4 tbsp strawberry jam
1 tbsp icing sugar, to dust

1 Preheat the oven to 200°C/400°F/Gas Mark 6. Lightly grease four individual deep ramekin dishes with the butter. Put the dishes into a medium roasting tin with 1inch of water.
2 Whisk the egg whites in a clean, dry bowl until stiff, then whisk in the sugar, a spoonful at a time, until it is thick and glossy. Fold in the jam, then spoon the soufflé mixture into the prepared ramekin dishes.
3 Bake on a centre shelf in the preheated oven for 12-15 mins.
4 Lightly dust with the icing sugar and serve immediately.
© www.bonnemaman.co.uk

4	Monday

5	Tuesday

6	Wednesday

7	Thursday

8	Friday

9	Saturday

10	Sunday

Blast from the past

Jennifer in charge of her dad's tame rams

Dad was a shepherd

In 1958 I lived with Mum and Dad in a primitive cottage on the common at Maund Bryan, Bodenham in Herefordshire. It had a tin roof, no electricity, a well and a privy at the top of the garden. Dad was a shepherd. Although my parents didn't have much money, for me it was idyllic because I had the freedom of the common to play on – I'm with two of my dad's tame rams Billie and Charlie in the photo. There was a stream where my sister and I collected frogspawn and picked wild watercress.

Once a year, in summertime, the 'donkey man' arrived on the common with a cart pulled by a donkey. We never knew his name and he never stopped for more than a few days. He had a dog, a monkey and white mice and when we went to see him he would get the monkey to do little tricks. Then I would wake up one morning and he would be gone until next year. Periodically, Romanies would camp on the common, doing seasonal work like hop picking. I would look out of my window and see them all sat around a campfire at night. They had brightly painted caravans with rounded roofs and they would graze their horses on the common. Looking back, it seemed like a whole different world to today.

Jennifer Phillipson, Hereford

What a good idea!

During the hot, sunny weather, you might find that dark clothes tend to start fading on the washing line in the direct light of the sun. So turn any coloured clothes inside out before you hang them on the line. You'll find the colour keeps much better, meaning your clothes will last longer.

C Davies, Cornwall

Quick brain boost

Can you crack the code? If S=W, E=I and J=N what does SDENHSEJZO say? Answer below

Garden inspiration

PIC: ALAMY

Jobs for July

◆ Clip fast-growing hedges such as privet and Lonicera nitida. Hawthorn hedge can be trimmed now.
◆ Plant autumn-flowering bulbs such as crocus, colchicum, Amaryllis belladonna and Nerine bowdenii
◆ Divide bearded irises towards the end of the month.
◆ Summer prune apple, plum and pear trees.
◆ In a dry spell, water runner beans and salad crops regularly.
◆ Feed tomato plants and nip out all side shoots.
◆ Start to harvest carrots and beetroot.
◆ Give wisterias a summer prune by cutting back the long whippy side growths to about four leaves from the main stem.

Senior moments

I took my doorbell off the door so that I could bring it in and give it a good clean. But when I was in the middle of scrubbing it, I accidentally caught the bell and it rang. Immediately I rushed forward, anxious to catch the front door, only to remember that I had rung it myself.

Angela Patchett, Fleetwood

Quick brain boost answer: Whirlwinds
(each letter is shifted 3 letters down the alphabet)

Recipe of the week

BLUEBERRY YOGURT CHEESECAKE

Serves: 4
Preparation time: 15 mins
Soaking time: 4 hours
Setting time: 1–2 hours

500g (1lb2oz) Alpro Simply Plain
150g (5oz) of blueberries
3 leaves of gelatine
100g (4oz) macadamia nuts
50g (2oz) medjool dates
10g (^{1}/₂oz) desiccated coconut

1 Place the macadamia nuts in a bowl and cover with cold water, leave to soak for 4 hrs.
2 Drain the remaining water and place in a food processor adding the dates to the mixture until you have a fine crumb consistency.
3 Take four small ring moulds or ramekins and sprinkle with the desiccated coconut, spoon in the macadamia nut crumbs and spread across the base, evenly pressing down with the back of a spoon.
4 Break the gelatine leaves into small pieces and soak in a tbsp of cold water for 5 mins to soften and then heat in a microwave on a hob until dissolved
5 Place the Alpro and the blueberries in a food processor and blend until smooth before adding the liquid gelatine.
6 Pour the blueberry yogurt mixture on top of the macadamia nut bases and place in the fridge to set. When set, carefully remove the ring moulds and serve.

© www.alpro.com

11	Monday
12	Tuesday
13	Wednesday
14	Thursday
15	Friday
16	Saturday
17	Sunday

Blast from the past

A snapshot taken in **Margate** led to a screen surprise

As seen on screen

In the Thirties, my parents sometimes managed to afford a week's holiday in Margate. It had everything a child could wish for – lovely beach, a pier, the Dreamland funfair and colourful shops on the seafront selling buckets and spades, flags for sandcastles, sweets and sticks of rock. We used to catch the coach near our home in north west London, passing through the narrow streets of Canterbury on the way. My brother and I always tried to be the first one to see the sea. During our holiday, there was always the beach photographer going around the beach or along the promenade, trying to persuade people to have a photo taken. You could view them on a kiosk on the promenade the next day and, if you liked it, could buy it.

When we were back home, we used to love going to the local cinema on a Saturday morning for the children's film show. Unbeknown to us, my mother had submitted our holiday snaps into a competition at the cinema. You can imagine our surprise when, during the interval the winning photos were shown on the large screen and there was my brother and I. All our friends cheered. I have no idea if there was a prize, but the memory is still there, even if we are both in our 80s. **Gordon Carter, York**

What a good idea!

If you find white flies trouble your vegetable crops in the summer, plant some mint between each line of vegetables. The white flies hate the smell of the mint so they stay away. I originally thought this was just an old wives' tale but it really kept my vegetables insect-free all year. **Maureen Gribe, Lancaster**

Quick brain boost

Can you unscramble this anagram to make an 11-letter word?

LAIR NET QUIZ

Answer below

Garden inspiration

In bloom now: stately delphiniums

No cottage garden is complete without blue delphiniums towering majestically above the lupins, geraniums and dianthus. As well as a stunning spectrum of blues, there are pink, cream and mauve spires to add colour to mid-summer borders. While the Pacific hybrids and delphinium elatum give us blooms that grow up to eight or nine feet tall, they require firm staking if they are to survive summer breezes. The belladonna strain of delphiniums grows to a more manageable four foot in height with 'Atlantis' being especially recommended for its dark blue hue.

Senior moments

I was cleaning my windows when I realised, after ten minutes, that they weren't getting any cleaner. In fact they looked more streaked than ever. It was then that I realised I was only trying to clean my windows with Vanish. The bottle was the same shape as my window cleaner. After finally using the right bottle, the results were spectacular.

Mrs S A Ringer, Cambridgeshire

Quick brain boost answer: Tranquilize

Recipe of the week

HOT & SWEET MANGO PRAWN SALAD

Serves: 4
Preparation time: 5 mins
Cooking time: 5 mins

400g (14oz) large raw tiger prawns
1 tbsp Groovy Food Virgin Coconut Oil
100g (4oz) dried vermicelli rice noodles
1 red pepper, deseeded and sliced
1 green pepper, deseeded and sliced
1 red onion, sliced thinly
1 large carrot, julienned
100g (4oz) sugar snap peas, sliced lengthways
1 slightly under-ripe mango, peeled and julienned
1 red chilli, deseeded and sliced
Fresh coriander to garnish
Dressing:
1 tbsp Groovy Food Agave Nectar Rich and Dark
1 tbsp soy sauce
2 tbsp Groovy Food High Five Oil
$1/2$ clove garlic crushed
Juice 1 lime

1 Cook the noodles by placing into a bowl and pouring over boiling water, leave to stand for 5 mins then drain and leave to cool. Meanwhile prepare the vegetables and set aside in a large bowl.
2 Preheat a frying pan then add in the coconut oil, fry the prawns for 2-3 mins per side, until pink and cooked through.
3 Meanwhile whisk together the dressing for the salad. Finally dress the noodles, peppers, carrot, red onion, beansprouts, sugar snaps, mango and chilli serve up topped with the hot prawns then garnish with the coriander.
©www.groovyfood.co.uk

18 Monday

19 Tuesday

20 Wednesday

21 Thursday

22 Friday

23 Saturday

24 Sunday

Blast from the past

Jill proudly showing off her handbag to her grandma

Memories of my wonderful Grandma

My grandma was blind, but she didn't let that stop her from cooking cakes, pies, stews and roasts. She made rhubarb, gooseberry and elderberry wines from fruit in her garden. We shared a birthday – April 18, she was born in 1886, I in 1946. I loved to draw her pictures in thick crayons so that she could 'see' them with her hands – which she did, carefully running her fingers over the house, the flowers, and the big yellow smiley sun in the top, right-hand corner. "That's beautiful," she would say and place it on her mantelpiece. In the photo I am proudly showing her my new handbag (I was eight at the time) and thought it looked like the Queen's.

She loved silk blouses and we would tidy her bedroom drawers, feeling the shimmery fabric. Each blouse was identified with a tiny gilt safety pin. She never forgot which was which! She used to leave a can of Nestlé's condensed milk opened in her pantry. Little fingers were often dipped in and sucked with sugary delight. It was not until I was 25 that I realised that she had left it there on purpose. "It tastes even better when it's pinched, doesn't it?" she said, laughing. A lovely lady. I adored her.

Jill Friendship, Bristol

What a good idea!

When I go on holiday, I always pack two hair clips with me that I fasten to the top corners of my newspapers and books. This keeps the pages in place when there's a breeze so that I can sit on the beach and read without all the pages blowing in my face.

Lena Waites, County Durham

Quick brain boost

Garden inspiration

PIC: SHUTTERSTOCK

Great garden tip

If ants are a pest, try spreading a liberal amount of cayenne pepper around the base of any plants that need protection. Alternatively, baking yeast mixed with a sugar solution spread on pieces of bark placed around the roots of a tree should prevent them climbing up the trunk. Plants that are disliked by ants include lavender, African marigold, pot marigold, pennyroyal and chives, so it is a good idea to plant them as a repellent in a part of the garden that is particularly affected by these insects.

Senior moments

The other day I was trying to find Sammy Squirrel in my copy of **Yours** magazine, as always. In the end I gave up and instead made a start on reading my morning paper. After a few minutes I realised that I was still scouring each page looking for Sammy Squirrel in there. Silly me!

Mrs P Hatch, Preston

Quick brain boost answer:
A living man shouldn't be buried anywhere!

Recipe of the week

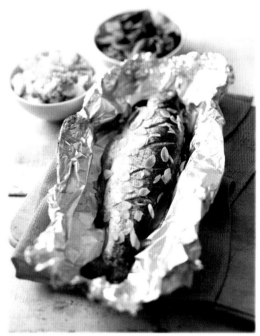

BAKED TROUT WITH ALMONDS

Serves: 2
Preparation time: 5 mins
Cooking time: 15 mins

2 rainbow trout, cleaned
25g (1oz) flaked almonds
1 tbsp olive oil
Zest of $1/2$ lemon
20g ($3/4$oz) spreadable butter or margarine
160g (5oz) spring greens
200g (7oz) new potatoes
Pinch of black pepper
Fresh dill or parsley to garnish

1 Preheat the oven to 200°C/400°F/Gas Mark 6.
2 Lightly grease two pieces of foil with half the olive oil. Lay the trout on the greased foil and make three to four diagonal slashes through the skin. Rub the trout with the remaining oil, then sprinkle the lemon zest and almonds.
3 Create a parcel out of foil containing the fish and bake for 15 mins until the fish flakes easily.
4 While the parcels are cooking, steam the spring greens and boil the new potatoes in unsalted water. Drain both.
5 Lightly crush new potatoes with the butter and black pepper.
6 Serve the trout (with or without parcel juices) with crushed potatoes and greens and garnish with fresh herbs.

©www.flora.com

25 Monday

26 Tuesday

27 Wednesday

28 Thursday

29 Friday

30 Saturday

31 Sunday

Blast from the past

Helen in her crêpe hula hula fancy-dress outfit

Fun to stay at the YMCA

All my family went to Barry Island in Wales for their holidays – aunts, uncles and cousins. It began just after the war when we stayed at a boarding house in Barry town – the landlady's name was Mrs Grant. As our family grew we moved to the YMCA at Cold Knap, a small, pebbled beach about 15 minutes from Barry – and we stayed there every year until I was about 12 years old. Staying at the YMCA meant we had to adhere to some rules and regulations. For example, doors closed at 11pm, alcohol was not permitted and grace was sung before every meal.

Each week they held a fancy dress competition for both children and adults. Costumes were very amateur – not like they are today. They were either made from crêpe paper, as my hula hula girl costume was in the photo, or put together from such things as sheets and towels. Otherwise you could always go as a tramp – the good old standby! When I was 17 I was allowed to holiday with my friend for the first time without my family. But only on the condition that we went to the YMCA. They knew I could not come to much harm there.

Mrs Helen Haden, Solihull

What a good idea!

This is an easy way to make a good greenfly deterrent spray for your plants. Just boil a handful of nettles (using gloves so you don't get stung) in a pint of water and then put this liquid in a spray bottle. If you leave the nettles to soak for a few days this also makes a great fertiliser for your garden.

Louie Bancroft, Newcastle

What comes next in this number sequence?

97, 90, 84, 79, 75, 72, ??

Answer below

Garden inspiration

PIC: ANN FRASER

Visit Shepherd House Garden

Proof that small is beautiful, Shepherd House Garden in the village of Inveresk in East Lothian measures only one acre but contains fountains, parterres, an alpine wall, a potager and a woodland. A formal rill runs the length of the walled garden, linking two ponds. Ann Fraser, who created the garden with her husband, is an artist who finds inspiration for her work in the flowers around her. A recent addition is a shell house with stained glass windows depicting some of the plants that grow in the garden.
Email ann@shepherdhousegarden.co.uk or call 0131 665 2570

Senior moments

When my grandma came back from holiday, she decided the first thing she fancied was a long, hot bath. While the water was running, she poured into the bath a sachet she'd brought back from the hotel room. It was only once she'd got in that she noticed the water looked a strange colour and realised she was actually bathing in hot chocolate.

Charlotte Waters, Burnley

Quick brain boost answer: **70** (the rule is -7, -6, -5 etc)

Recipe of the week

STRAWBERRY & ORANGE FOOL

Serves: 6
Preparation time: 10 mins
Chilling time: 1 hour

400g (14oz) strawberries (with a few extra for garnish)
Juice of one orange
1-2 drops of orange essence (optional)
300ml (10½floz) double cream
300ml (10½floz) thick Greek yogurt
100g (4oz) icing sugar
1 tbsp caster sugar

1 Wash and chop the strawberries, keeping some aside for the garnish. Place the chopped strawberries in a bowl, roughly mash them up and fold in the orange juice and orange essence (if using) and the icing sugar.
2 In a separate bowl, whip the cream until stiff peaks form and then gently fold in the yogurt and finally the strawberry mixture. Pour into 6 glasses and chill for a least 1 hour.
3 Just before serving, take the reserved strawberries, cut in half and roll the pointed ends in the caster sugar before arranging the two halves on the top of the fool.
©www.sweetevestrawberry.co.uk

1 Monday

2 Tuesday

3 Wednesday

4 Thursday

5 Friday

6 Saturday

7 Sunday

Blast from the past

Marion's first Boys' Brigade camp was at three months old

At Boys' Brigade camp

As a child I went to Boys' Brigade camping holidays for one week every August – even though I was a girl. And it was my best holiday ever. My father was an officer – later the captain of the 1st Colchester Company and wives and children were allowed to go to camp too. I was born in June and my first camp was at age three months! We travelled by charabanc, which was great fun, and joined many other Boys' Brigade companies at the seaside town of Walton-on-the-Naze in Essex. There could be as many as 300 of us, all in bell tents. As well as breakfast we had two hot, cooked meals a day which were served in big marquees. We played games, had a sports day and spent days on the beach swimming.

The boys ranged in age from ten to 18 years and had a parade every morning before relaxing, plus we all went to the local church on the Sundays. I went to camp for ten years and it always seemed to be hot. I am 90 now but looking back they were the best holidays ever.

Marion Ward, Essex

What a good idea!

Don't throw away the clear plastic bags that your bread comes in. Instead keep a stash of them in your kitchen to put your filled rolls in when you're doing a packed lunch. Your sandwiches will stay nice and fresh in there, but you won't have to buy so many plastic sandwich bags.

Carol Casan, Tiverton

Quick brain boost

Can you crack the code? If J=E, T=O and X=S what does ATQZSYJJWX say?

Answer below

Garden inspiration

Jobs for August

◆ Water lawns during any dry spells. Apply weedkiller if needed.
◆ Plant Madonna lilies (Lilium candidum) in a sunny, well-drained situation.
◆ Pick peas, beans and courgettes regularly.
◆ Dig up onions and spread on the ground to dry before storing.
◆ Take semi-hard or softwood cuttings from rockery plants such as thyme, dianthus, genista and helianthemum.
◆ Collect ripe seeds from fennel and dill for resowing.
◆ Take semi-ripe cuttings from shrubs such as cornus, buddleia and philadelphus.
◆ Deadhead hydrangeas, removing any weak stems.
◆ Make time to relax in your garden and enjoy the bounty of high summer.

Senior moments

I hadn't been very well and had visited various consultants with different complaints. Anyway, recently I went for a hospital appointment and was waiting for more than an hour when I lost my patience. I asked the receptionist if they had forgotten me and when she checked, it turned out I had the right date, right time, wrong hospital! What a moment!

Margaret Brothwood, West Midlands

Quick brain boost answer: Volunteers
(each letter is shifted 5 letters up the alphabet)

Recipe of the week

SMOKED SALMON SALAD

Serves: 4
Preparation time: 10 mins
Cooking time: 2 mins

150g (5oz) sugar snaps
1 avocado
1 lemon, juiced
200g (7oz) artichokes in oil, drained
400g (14oz) hot smoked salmon, flaked
2 spring onions, sliced
50g (2oz) radishes, sliced
Small bunch of dill, chopped
2 tbsp mayonnaise
Salt and pepper

1 Bring a small pan of salted water to the boil and cook the sugar snaps for 2 mins, drain and refresh under cold water for 1 min, then set aside.
2 Cut the avocado in half, then remove the stone and scoop out the flesh, then cut into chunks. Place the avocado into a medium-sized bowl with the lemon juice.
3 Cut the artichokes into chunks and add to the avocado, then add the sugar snaps, salmon, spring onions, radishes, dill and mayonnaise, season with salt and pepper, gently mix and divide between 4 bowls.
© o-liveorganic.com

8 Monday

9 Tuesday

10 Wednesday

11 Thursday

12 Friday

13 Saturday

14 Sunday

Blast from the past

Ann, left, with her cousin Janet in 1963.

Fun with my fabulous cousin

As a teenager I was living in London and my family could never afford holidays. However, I had a cousin, Janet, the same age as me so each summer I was sent off to her house in Stevenage for two weeks. It was the highlight of my year. Stevenage was then a new town and was surrounded by countryside. How I used to envy them their brand new council house and large garden. My aunt used to take us to Knebworth Park to pick berries and climb trees. One of my funniest memories is Janet and I up our favourite tree (which we called The Rocket) laughing as my aunt tried to shoo away an inquisitive herd of cows.

Janet was a lot more mature than I was and took me to my first dance hall, The Mecca. She produced a lipstick for us to wear but we had to wipe it off before my uncle picked us up. When two boys asked us to dance, Janet was straight on to the dance floor. My response was to rush to the bathroom in tears as I didn't know what to do! My aunt baked, made jams and made all Janet's clothes. I thought that was fabulous as I only ever had hand-me-downs. It was only later when we were adults that Janet admitted she had envied me those hand-me-downs. She thought shop-bought clothes were much more sophisticated.

Miss Ann Rowe, London

What a good idea!

My butcher recently gave me a great tip for keeping flies away from the kitchen and my food, especially in the hot weather. Just keep a few sprigs of parsley in a cup of water on the kitchen windowsill. The flies are deterred by the smell of the parsley so they don't bother you anymore.

Violet Taylor, London

Quick brain boost

Can you unscramble this anagram to make an 11-letter word?
VIA COY QUELL   Answer below

Garden inspiration

PIC: ALAMY

In bloom now: razzle-dazzle dahlias

Bursting with vibrant colour, dahlias are not for faint-hearted souls who like subtle, understated flower borders. Once out of fashion, dahlias came back with a bang when gardeners discovered the Bishop of Llandaff with its elegant scarlet flowers contrasting with dark purple foliage. The dahlia's popularity has gone from strength to strength as gardeners discovered its amazing variety of forms, ranging from the shaggy cactuses to neat single-flowered types, in every colour imaginable. Best of all, dahlias need nothing more than regular deadheading to keep flowering right through to autumn.

Senior moments

When I was buying a new laptop, the computer salesman in the shop asked me: "Would you like us to install any parental controls on the PC for you?" I straight away replied: "No, it's okay, thank you, I don't have any parents." Needless to say, he looked rather puzzled at me.

Maureen Parry, County Antrim

Quick brain boost answer: Equivocally

Recipe of the week

CHOCOLATE AND PISTACHIO PAVLOVA

Serves: 8
Prep: 25 mins
Cook: 1¼ hours

4 medium egg whites
225g (8oz) caster sugar
40g (1½ oz) pistachio nuts, very finely chopped
100g (4oz) dark chocolate, broken into pieces
300ml (½ pt) double cream
550g (1lb 2oz) mixed strawberries, hulled, halved, blackberries, blueberries and raspberries

1 Preheat the oven to 140°C/275°F/Gas Mark 1. Line a baking sheet with non-stick baking paper and draw a 23cm (9in) circle on to it.
2 Whisk the egg whites until they form stiff peaks.
3 Gradually whisk in the sugar a tsp at a time and continue whisking once all the sugar has been added, whisk for a few more mins until the meringue is thick and glossy.
4 Fold in the pistachio nuts. Spoon the meringue inside the marked circle on the baking sheet and spread into soft swirls. Bake for 1¼ hours until crisp on the outside.
5 Leave the pavlova to cool still on the paper, on a wire rack.
6 Melt the chocolate in a bowl set over a saucepan of simmering water. Lift the pavlova off the paper on to a serving plate then drizzle the chocolate over the top.
7 Whip the cream until it forms soft swirls then spoon over the chocolate-topped pavlova. Scatter the berries on top and serve.

©www.seasonalberries.co.uk

15 Monday

16 Tuesday

17 Wednesday

18 Thursday

19 Friday

20 Saturday

21 Sunday

Blast from the past

Going for a picnic ended in a memorable journey home

The bare essentials?

When I was about ten years old, Dad and Mam took my sister Margaret, her friend and myself out for a picnic. Mam told me to take my shorts off if I wanted to paddle in the river. I refused point blank as I wasn't going to let anyone see me just in my knickers. Of course, it wasn't long before I slipped and fell down in the river, soaking everything. So I had to strip off and put my coat on. Dad had just finished hanging the clothes on a tree when Margaret did a repeat performance. Luckily we had brought coats and not jackets with us. By now, Mam and Dad decided they had had enough, so after a quick picnic we returned home in the car.

Margaret held one pair of pants out of one window while her friend held a pair out at the other side. I knelt up to watch for any approaching traffic, shouting, 'knickers in, knickers out, knickers in, knickers out'. Luckily there were not many cars about 60 years ago. And not only was our day cut short but my shorts had to be thrown out as Mam couldn't get them clean.

Mrs Doreen Duguid, Darlington

What a good idea!

When I'm gardening, I warm up the water in my watering can by leaving it in the direct sunlight just for a few minutes. This means the water isn't as much of a shock to your plants as ice cold water would be, keeping young bedding plants much happier and so more successful all summer through.

Carole Gasan, Gloucestershire

Quick brain boost

Can you solve this riddle?
A football fan claimed to be able to tell the score before any game. How did he do it? Answer below

Garden inspiration

PIC: SHUTTERSTOCK

Great garden tip

To water deep-rooted plants effectively in a dry spell of weather, bury a length of one-inch metal or rubber piping next to a newly planted tree or shrub. Leave a good inch of piping above the ground so that a bucket of water can be poured in via a funnel. This is more effective than watering the ground around the plant as this only soaks into the top layer of soil, thus encouraging the roots to grow towards the surface where they risk being scorched in a hot summer.

Senior moments

I was on holiday in Singapore on a river cruise when I spotted a sign that read 'ixat'. "What a lovely exotic word," I said to my friend. "I wonder what it means?" It was then that my friend gently pointed out to me that we were sailing past the back of the taxi rank. That gave me a bit of a clue!

Pamela Yarley, Worcester

Recipe of the week

FRUITY CINNAMON GRANOLA

Serves: 6
Preparation time: 5 mins
Cooking time: 15 mins

200g (7oz) whole rolled oats
150g (5oz) mixed nuts, seed and berries (we used pumpkin seeds, sunflower seeds, pine nuts, dried cranberries and goji berries)
50g (2oz) almonds, crushed
2 tbsp chia seeds
40g (1½oz) dried apricots, finely chopped
2 tbsp Groovy Food Virgin Coconut Oil
1 tsp ground cinnamon
40g (1½oz) Groovy Food Agave Nectar Light and Mild

1 In a small pan gently warm the coconut oil until melted. Meanwhile combine the dry ingredients in a bowl then add the agave nectar and oil then stir until fully combined.
2 Spread on to a greased baking tray and bake in a preheated oven set at 180°C/350°F/Gas Mark 4 for 10-15 mins.
3 Remove from the oven and leave to cool before crumbling into an airtight container.
4 Serve with some fresh berries, Greek yogurt and another drizzle of agave if you like.
© www.groovyfood.co.uk

22 Monday

23 Tuesday

24 Wednesday

25 Thursday

26 Friday

27 Saturday

28 Sunday

Blast from the past

Velma, left, with Win

Our Festival weekend

The Festival of Britain opened on May 3, 1951 on London's South Bank and my friend Win and I, then in our teens, were eager to see it. At last, in August we were invited to stay for a weekend with her Aunt Emily and Uncle Sam who lived in Kentish Town in north London. We got to them on the Saturday morning and set off for the exhibition in the afternoon. The Dome of Discovery was the dominant feature, over which hovered the Skylon, looking like a giant aluminium exclamation mark. It was the symbol of the festival. As we mingled with the crowds, amid all the admiration, complaints could be heard about coffee costing 9d a cup! Imagine our excitement when later, on our way to a concert at the Royal Festival Hall in which Anton Dolan was the principal dancer, we caught a glimpse of the film stars Jack Hawkins and Constance Cummings...

Next morning we went on a walk with Emily and Sam, during which he pointed out places where, 'Jack the Ripper did one of 'em in'. We got as far as Westminster Abbey and ended in Sam's favourite pub before catching the afternoon train home. Sadly, Win is no longer here to share the memory of that enjoyable weekend.

Mrs Velma Wisher, Nottingham

What a good idea!

I've found the best way of separating egg yolk from the white is to use a saucer and egg cup. Just break the whole egg carefully on to the saucer and then put an egg cup over the yolk. Keeping the cup held down, you can then just pour off the egg white and the yolk can go elsewhere.

June Jones, Swansea

Quick brain boost

What comes next in this number sequence?

3, 9, 10, 30, 31, 93, ??

Answer below

Garden inspiration

PIC: ROGER VLITOS

Visit Buscot Park

The gardens that surround Buscot Park near Faringdon in Oxfordshire are on a grand scale that complements the handsome neo-classical house. Formerly a walled kitchen garden, the Four Seasons ornamental garden has been planted to provide year-round interest and in August visitors can enjoy many multi-coloured day lilies. Woodland walks lead to the splendid Italianate water garden that links the house to the Big Lake. Designed by Harold Peto more than a century ago, the water garden is flanked by box hedges, statues and terracotta jars.
Call 01367 240786

Senior moments

My daughter retired two months ago and I was telling my friends that her colleagues had given her a beautiful Durex watch as a retirement present. As I said this, I couldn't understand why they were all giving me a surprised look. Then one of them said: "I think you might mean a Rolex watch?"
Name withheld

Quick brain boost answer: **94 (the rule is x3, +1 etc)**

Recipe of the week

STEAK & BEETROOT SANDWICH

Serves: 2
Preparation time: 10 mins
Cooking time: 6 mins

2–3cm fat ribeye steak (approx 225g weight)
1 tbsp olive oil
Sea salt and freshly ground black pepper
2–4 shallots, finely sliced
2 beetroot balls, boiled for 40–45 mins and cut into slices
A few leaves of Cos Lettuce,
Ciabatta loaf, cut in half and sliced open
Salad dressing to serve

1 Heat the oil in a heavy-based frying pan until smoking hot. Season the steak on both sides. Lay the steak in the pan and fry, undisturbed, on one side for 2–3 mins. Flip over and fry on the other side for a further 2–3 mins. Remove the steak and allow to rest on a warm plate tightly covered in foil.
2 Add the shallots to the frying pan and fry for a few mins until softened and beginning to caramelise. Remove to a plate and keep warm.
3 Lay the ciabatta slices, cut side down, in the frying pan and toast lightly for a minute or two.
4 Place some torn lettuce leaves between 2 pieces of the ciabatta. Slice the steak into 1cm wide strips and arrange on top of the lettuce. Top with the sliced beetroot and fried onions. Finally drizzle over a little salad dressing.
© o-liveorganic.com

29	Monday

30	Tuesday

31	Wednesday

1	Thursday

2	Friday

3	Saturday

4	Sunday

Blast from the past

Magical memories of travelling around the countryside

Life with a travelling fair

I was born during the memorably long cold winter of 1947 when we lived in a caravan. What I first remember is riding my little red trike in a field while Dad was packing up the family-owned fair ready to go on the road to the next village. I was three years old and my sister was 20 – a big age gap. It really was a family business; my uncle and two aunts and their children, my granddad and grandmother travelled with us some of the time. We went to villages around Oxfordshire and Warwickshire during the summer months. My clever dad made a small roundabout by hand which he just pushed round, the little children loved it though. We all travelled in converted buses which had diesel engines and generators which also drove the lorries and the bigger fair rides. As well as the powered rides we had swingboats and side-stalls. I only went to school in the winter at the Oxfordshire village of Hook Norton. And that was where we also settled down after my parents sold the fair when I was ten years old.

Pam Ayres wrote a poem about our fair in the Seventies. It was called Madbrains Watkins and his travelling fair. She had remembered it from her childhood. It is lovely to think it was special to her too. I now live with my husband Michael in Banbury and own a touring caravan which we love going holidaying in.

Gill Whitehead, Banbury, Oxon

What a good idea!

Stains on white washing can be a real nightmare and proper stain removers aren't always cheap to buy. But I've found that a thriftier alternative is just to squirt on the stain a little sterilising liquid (you can buy this from most supermarkets as it's used for baby equipment) diluted in some water. It's an instant stain remover – but only on white fabrics.

Susan Rowley, Essex

Recipe of the week

Garden inspiration

PIC: ALAMY

Jobs for September

◆ Plant conifers, evergreen shrubs and trees. Support
with a stake against autumn gales.
◆ Take semi-hard cuttings of evergreens such as
holly and cherry laurel.
◆ Tie in new shoots on climbing roses.
Check for disease.
◆ Plant narcissi bulbs. Also pot up bulbs for winter
flowers indoors.
◆ Iris danfordiae and I histrioides can be planted
in pots and left in a cold frame for flowering
indoors later.
◆ Sow New Zealand spinach for picking through the
winter months.
◆ Lift pepper plants and hang upside down in a cool
dry place where peppers will continue to ripen.

Senior moments

I was going to stay with my son and my neighbour
kindly offered to drive me to the railway
station to get my train. Imagine my horror and
embarrassment when I realised, as I was getting
out of her car, about to wave goodbye, that I was
still wearing my slippers.

Enid Pitchers, Bristol

BLUEBERRY APPLE JELLIES

Serves: 4
Preparation time: 15 mins, plus 2–3 hours to set
Cooking time: None

300ml (½pt) blueberry juice 5 sheets of gelatine
300ml (½pt) sparkling apple juice
100g (4oz) fresh blueberries

1 Place the sheets of gelatine in a flat dish and
  sprinkle over 3 tbsp cold water. Leave to soak for
  3 mins until soft.
2 Squeeze the water out of the gelatine and place in
  a small pan and heat gently until melted.
3 Add the blueberry juice and sparkling apple juice
  and mix thoroughly.
4 Place a handful of fresh blueberries in the bottom
  of four glasses and pour over the jelly mix. Leave
  to set for 2–3 hours. Once set enjoy straight from
  the fridge.
©Ocean Spray®

September 5 - 11

5 Monday

6 Tuesday

7 Wednesday

8 Thursday

9 Friday

10 Saturday

11 Sunday

Blast from the past

The retirement tea. Priscilla is kneeling on the far right

Life as a school librarian

Entering Ashford Grammar in 1949, I was impressed with the library, situated upstairs. When I was old enough to join I did, and became an avid reader. Frequently I researched homework there, enjoying the silence. In the sixth form we had study periods which we spent in the library. My keenness was observed and I became a librarian, rising to head librarian in 1955. The master librarian outlined my duties. We had to keep the library tidy, issue books, classify new books in the Dewey system, then shelve them. It was a busy, if silent, place – with only some conversation after school when routine tasks were finished.

The spring term began and we learnt that the library would relocate to larger premises in the summer holidays. This was needed – but it wouldn't feel the same. With my A-levels ahead I concentrated on keeping the library ticking over, plus studying. Once the exams were over we planned the move, understanding we needed to work in our holidays and happy to do so.

After school was finished, we packed books to be taken to the new area downstairs. Well-worn, old volumes were removed and we were allowed to keep some of them. With regret we left the old library to the builders. We ex-librarians enjoyed a 'retirement' tea at my home – happy that we would all be elsewhere in September.

Mrs Priscilla J Odell, Middx

What a good idea!

I have very sensitive skin, so I struggle to wear earrings that don't irritate my ears. But I've found that if I rub just a little Vaseline on the hook or the stud of the earring, this stops the problem. My ears no longer get inflamed and I can enjoy wearing earrings again.

Nina Bradshaw, Manchester

Quick brain boost

Garden inspiration

PIC ALAMY

In bloom now: dainty anemones

Hailing originally from the Orient, Japanese
anemones have an irresistible exotic beauty – but
don't be deceived because they can turn into thugs
that thrust their way up through paving stones and
are difficult to eradicate. Planted in an area such as
a wild garden where they can happily spread, they
bloom through the autumn months and have the
added virtue of being deer-resistant. 'September
Charm' has pretty rose-pink flowers while 'Honorine
Jobert' is a pure white form and 'Queen Charlotte' has
semi-double flowers that are an unusual silvery pink.

Senior moments

I was on the phone to my nephew when he offered
to come round to do some weeding in my garden for
me. "That would be lovely," I said. "But please don't
come on Wednesday. I have to attend the antenatal
clinic." I didn't realise until he burst out laughing
that I'd meant to say the anticoagulant clinic. I'm 84.

Barbra Hill, Surrey

Quick brain boost answer: Lumberjacks

Recipe of the week

CLOTTED CREAM RICE PUDDING

Serves: 4–5
Preparation time: 10 mins
Cooking time: 1½ hour

Knob of butter
1 litre (1¾ pint) Jersey or whole milk
50g (2oz) golden caster sugar
1 vanilla pod slit lengthwise
110g (4oz) short grain pudding rice
6 tbsps clotted cream
Freshly grated nutmeg
Jam to serve

1 Preheat the oven to 150°C/300°F/Gas Mark 2.
2 Grease a medium–sized ovenproof dish with
   butter. Pour the milk into a saucepan, add the
   caster sugar and the seeds the vanilla pod and
   stir together over a low heat until the sugar has
   dissolved.
3 Add the rice and bring to the boil, reduce the heat
   and simmer for a few mins until the rice starts to
   swell.
4 Stir in the clotted cream and when the cream
   has completely melted, pour the mixture into the
   prepared ovenproof dish.
5 Dot the top of the pudding with a little extra butter
   and grate a generous amount of nutmeg on top.
6 Cook the pudding in the preheated oven for 1½
   hours, until the top is golden brown and the rice
   is soft.
©Recipe from Comfort by Carolyn Caldicott, Frances Lincoln, £9.99.

12 Monday

13 Tuesday

14 Wednesday

15 Thursday

16 Friday

17 Saturday

18 Sunday

Blast from the past

Jean with her granny at the allotments

When tears meant treats

I was born in North Yorkshire in 1939. Dad died when I was just four years old and it was hard for Mam, but the family made sure 'little Jean' didn't go without, so I was quite spoilt. My grandparents lived close by and I can still remember the fantastic food Granny cooked on the range – rice pudding, bread and casseroles. And I loved going to the allotment with her.

Mam managed to get a job as housekeeper at the old Hall next to Ripon Cathedral. This was owned by the Oxley Family – Admiral Charles Oxley and his sister, Agnes. One day while sitting in the drawing room I was stung by a wasp. It was quite comical as Agnes immediately blamed Charles saying: "They're your bees." Charles replied: "No, you silly woman it was one of your knitting needles." Seeing my tears their solution was to get the gardener to bring 'the child' some strawberries. I was soon to find out that a few tears always brought 'the child' various treats – peaches from the hothouse, chocolates and so on. One vivid memory was the large brown bear at the top of the stairs. It scared me silly! There were also several stuffed animal heads and a tiger rug. Oh, what lovely memories!   **Mrs J Whiston, Preston**

What a good idea!

This treatment for warts might have come from a book of old wives' tales, but I found it genuinely worked for me. Just squeeze out the milk from the inside of a dandelion stem and apply this to your wart every day. After a couple of weeks of doing this, the wart will drop off completely.
Susan Nightingale, Cornwall

Quick brain boost

Can you solve this riddle?
What word describes a woman who does not have all her fingers on one hand?   Answer below

Garden inspiration

PIC: ALAMY

Great garden tip

Before planting spring-flowering bulbs, soak them for thirty minutes in a solution of one tablespoon of paraffin to 600ml of water to prevent rabbits and squirrels digging them up and eating them. If you are especially plagued by rabbits, try creating a bed of plants that they dislike such as Geranium macrorrhizum 'Walter Ingwersen' combined with very thorny species of roses. Herbs such as basil, chives, rosemary and sage are also unattractive to rabbits. A scattering of Epsom salts should keep them away from vulnerable plants such as dianthus.

Senior moments

The doctor was examining my eye three weeks after I'd had a cataract operation. "Do you think there's been an improvement?" he asked me. Excitedly, I replied: "It's marvellous. I opened the curtains this morning and saw the pears on my apple tree for the very first time." The doctor told me that he knew the operation was good, but didn't realise it could perform miracles.

Edna Wilde, Worcester

Quick brain boost answer: Normal – you shouldn't have all 10 fingers on one hand

Recipe of the week

POSH FISH & CHIPS

450g (1lb) sweet potatoes, peeled and cut into chips
2 tbsp vegetable oil
85g (3oz) slightly stale bread
4 tbsp fresh chopped parsley
4x175g (6oz) fish fillets, e.g. cod, plaice
Zest of 1 lemon
1 tbsp plain flour
1 medium egg, beaten
For the mushy peas:
225g (8oz) frozen peas
40g (1½oz) spreadable butter or margarine
1 tbsp fresh mint leaves, chopped
1 to 2 tbsp low-fat natural yogurt

1 Preheat oven to 200°C/400°F/Gas Mark 6.
2 Toss the chips in half the oil and spread evenly over a baking sheet. Bake in the oven for 40 mins.
3 Meanwhile prepare the fish by placing the bread, half the parsley and lemon zest in a food processor and blitz until rough breadcrumbs.
4 Stir through a tablespoon of oil.
5 Place flour, egg, and crumbs on separate plates and dunk each fillet in flour, then egg, finishing with the crumbs. Place on a non-stick baking sheet and bake for the last 12 mins of chips' cooking time.
6 While the fish is cooking, cook the peas in boiling water for 4 mins, drain and mash with the butter, mint and remaining parsley and lemon zest.
7 Add the yogurt to achieve a soft consistency and serve with the fish and chips.
©www.flora.com

19	Monday
20	Tuesday
21	Wednesday
22	Thursday
23	Friday
24	Saturday
25	Sunday

Blast from the past

Ruth, fifth from the left, on the second row

My old dependable friend

Typewriters have always been in my life. From 1944 to 1946 I attended Folkestone Technical School (that's my class in the photo) where the most important lesson was typewriting. Some 25 girls pounded away on heavy machines, with the keyboards covered by metal shields so that we learned to touch type. Frequently, the typing exercises were accompanied by loud, steady and rhythmic music and we would strike the keys in time to a measured beat of the simple tune. At the end of each line of the exercise a voice would boom out the instruction, 'carriage return'.

My working life started with an old, dependable Imperial 66. In 1951, when I was 21, my parents bought me my own typewriter. Gouldens of Canterbury, Typewriter Specialists, supplied my portable, shiny model with its strong carrying case. Called Everest, it was made in Italy, with Mod.90 emblazoned above its keyboard. Known affectionately by me as 'Little Everest', he was finally replaced in 1980. I couldn't bear to part with him, and ever since he has had a place of honour on the top of a chest of drawers, a constant reminder of loyalty and a lifetime of hard service spanning nearly 65 years.

Ruth Spencer, Kent

What a good idea!

Hanging baskets often look so sad once the flowers in them have died off come autumn time. But I've found a great way to keep your baskets still looking lovely right through the cold months. Just fill it with some pine cones – it looks rather effective and takes no looking after at all. Works great for winter.

Lisa Wright, North Devon

Quick brain boost

Garden inspiration

PIC: FRED CHOLMELEY

Visit Easton Walled Gardens

Designed with children as well as grown-ups in mind, Easton Walled Gardens in Lincolnshire feature a yew tunnel, a birdhide, a turf maze and a swing. The 12 acres have been owned by the Cholmeley family for 400 years but fell into disuse after the house was pulled down. Restoration began in 2001 and visitors can now stroll round a woodland walk, The Pickery (a cutflower garden, pictured) and a traditional cottage garden. More than 100 varieties of sweet peas are grown here and sweet pea seeds are sold in the shop.
Visit www.eastonwalledgardens.co.uk or call 01476 530063

Senior moments

I noticed that our bathroom door hinge was starting to squeak, so I told my husband about it. "Don't worry," he said. "I'll just go and spray some UB40 on the hinge." We both giggled when we realised he, in fact, meant WD40. It may have made a nicer noise actually if he had used UB40.

Jean Davies, Edinburgh

Quick brain boost answer: **89** (the rule is: +4,+8,+12,+16 etc)

Recipe of the week

CORNISH SAFFRON BUNS

Serves: 12
Preparation time: 10 mins
Cooking time: 20 mins

285ml (½ pt) semi-skimmed milk
½ tsp saffron strands
340g (12oz) self-raising flour
½ tsp salt
55g (2oz) unsalted butter
85g (3oz) caster sugar
200g (7oz) currants
2 large eggs, lightly beaten

1 Preheat the oven to 190°C/375°F/Gas Mark 5 and line a 12-hole muffin tray with paper cases or squares of baking paper.
2 Put the milk and saffron into a pan and warm gently. Remove from the heat and leave to infuse while you get on with the rest of the recipe.
3 Put the flour and salt into a bowl and rub in the butter with your fingers; alternatively whizz in a food processor. Stir in the sugar and currants.
4 Pour the saffron milk through a sieve to strain and add to the mixture with the beaten eggs. Mix until combined and then spoon the mixture into the prepared cases.
5 Bake in the preheated oven for 20 mins. These are best enjoyed straight from the oven.
©Taken from Bake Me as Fast as You Can, by Miranda Gore, priced £14.99

26 Monday

27 Tuesday

28 Wednesday

29 Thursday

30 Friday

1 Saturday

2 Sunday

Blast from the past

First days at school

In 1947 I started at All Saints' School in Sidmouth, Devon. Mum walked me to and fro every day, one and a half miles each way, whatever the weather. The hours were nine until four and I had to stay to lunch, which was awful! I remember mash, cabbage, stew and semolina. We also had a third of a pint of milk mid-morning, which was frozen in the winter and too warm in summer. At assembly each morning we sang the hymn All Things Bright and Beautiful – I am still looking for a 'purple-headed fountain'! Being a quiet child, my favourite lesson was reading. At break-time we played playground games like, The alley, alley-oh, oranges and lemons, tag, hopscotch, chase, skipping, hide and seek. Once we put on a play about foreign countries and I was an Indian girl because I had long dark hair. I hated doing it because I was so shy, but had to say, 'I come from India's sunny land, a fragrant garland in my hand'. I was so petrified and yet I can remember it to this day (and I'm now 72)! In the photo I am three rows back on the left with dark hair and a slide.

Mrs Hazel Clapp, Devon

What a good idea!

When you keep all your jewellery together in a box, it's easy for them to get knotted and tied together. You can unravel these knots more easily and with less risk of damaging them by first sprinkling them with a little talcum powder before teasing out the snags. This even works for your fine jewellery.

Shirley Dickens, Worcestershire

Quick brain boost

Can you crack the code? **If W=T, A=A and J=S what does WVATJSAWCJ say?**
Answer below

Garden inspiration

Jobs for October

PIC: SHUTTERSTOCK

◆ When cutting the lawn, increase the height of the mower blades.
◆ Plant deciduous shrubs and trees.
◆ Plant out spring cabbage.
◆ Prune rambler roses and take cuttings.
◆ Divide and replant overgrown perennials when they have finished flowering.
◆ Lift dahlias after the foliage has been blackened by frost. If leaving in the ground, protect with a thick mulch.
◆ Finish lifting root crops.
◆ Protect cauliflowers from early frosts.
◆ Clear fallen leaves from the pond and remove any dead water-lily leaves.
◆ Take hardwood cuttings of currant bushes and gooseberries.

Senior moments

As I was coming out of a shop last week, I was passing a column in the shopping arcade when I saw someone coming towards me. So I swiftly moved aside to get out of their way. At that moment I realised, to my confusion, that it was actually myself coming towards me in the long mirror on the column.

Jackie Downes, Chichester

Quick brain boost answer: Translates (complete the alphabet missing every other letter a=a, b=n, c=b etc)

Recipe of the week

OVEN-BAKED THAI COD

Serves: 4
Preparation time: 10 mins
Cooking time: 28 mins

1 tbsp Thai red curry paste
3 tbsp Flora Cuisine
Ground black pepper
4 cod fillets
1 onion, chopped
2 cloves garlic, chopped
115g (4oz) mushrooms, chopped
115g (4oz) cherry tomatoes

1 Preheat the oven to 190°C/375°F/Gas Mark 5.
2 Mix together Thai red curry paste with 2 tbsp Flora Cuisine and season with black pepper. Place the cod fillets in a lightly oiled oven dish and spread evenly with the curry paste mixture.
3 Heat remaining Flora Cuisine in a frying pan. Add in onions, garlic and mushrooms and fry for 3–5 mins until just softened. Spread this over the cod fillets and top with cherry tomatoes.
4 Bake for 25 mins, basting the fish now and then with the juices.
© www.flora.com

3 Monday

4 Tuesday

5 Wednesday

6 Thursday

7 Friday

8 Saturday

9 Sunday

Blast from the past

Dad the quiet hero

This is a picture of my dad during the Second World War in his London Auxiliary Fire Service uniform. As a child I was so proud and loved listening to his stories and was always asking him to tell me more. In many cases though they were quite upsetting and I think he really wanted to put it all behind him. Dad always kept a photo of St Paul's during the Blitz as he was actually there that dreadful night. A friend, who was an amateur artist, but who had also been in London during the war, asked if he could borrow it. He copied it and then gave it back to Dad and although it is not perfect it really captured the drama of the event. It still hangs on my wall today.

Many years later I was in London and went to visit St Paul's which was showing a special film that was dedicated to the many men and women responsible for saving the cathedral and London in general. You can imagine my surprise when suddenly I saw my beloved Dad up there on the screen. I came away feeling very proud and emotional.

Melanie Jackson, Dorset

Quick brain boost

Can you unscramble this anagram to make an 11-letter word?

EVICT JOY BIT

Answer below

Garden inspiration

PIC: SHUTTERSTOCK

In bloom now: Chinese plumbago

Providing a generous blaze of blue in the autumn garden, Chinese plumbago (Ceratostigma wilmottianum to give it its full name) prefers poor soil and is happiest in a sunny sheltered spot. The shrub's cobalt blue flowers nestle prettily among small leaves that take on a russet hue at this time of the year. Its herbaceous relation, Ceratostigma plumbaginoides, is a spreading, low-growing plant that gives good ground cover but can be invasive. Both types make a striking contrast when planted with the smoke bush Cotinus coggyria 'Royal Purple'.

Senior moments

I was having lunch with a friend when I noticed my false teeth were really hurting. I thought no more of it until the pain came back when I was eating dinner, at which point my husband commented that he'd also had trouble with his false teeth that day. Later, we discovered that we had been wearing each other's false teeth all day.　　　**Beryl Alsop, Buxton**

What a good idea!

For any budding artists looking for a cheap palette to use for painting, I've found a clever solution. Just head to your local discount store and look for a bargain ice tray. Usually they don't cost more than £1 and just do the trick for keeping and mixing your colours. Much cheaper than buying one at a proper art shop.

　　　Wendy Mallett, Suffolk

Quick brain boost answer: Objectivity

Recipe of the week

SQUASH, KALE & CHORIZO TORTILLA

Serves: 4
Preparation time: 5 mins
Cooking time: 15-18 mins

6 eggs, whisked up in a large bowl
2 tbsp olive oil or coconut oil
260g (9oz) cooking chorizo, sliced
2 plum tomatoes, diced
$\frac{1}{2}$ a butternut squash, diced into cubes
100g (4oz) kale, roughly chopped

1 Heat the oven to about 190°C/375°F/ Gas Mark 5.
2 Find a rectangular baking tray or dish about 20cm (8in) long with sides at least 5cm (2in) deep. Place dish in the oven to heat up while you get things cooking.
3 Fry the butternut squash in a non-stick pan using half the oil until it's almost cooked and golden brown — tip it into the bowl with the whisked eggs in. Leave the oil in the pan.
4 Fry the chorizo sausage until cooked and add to the egg mix — add the oil too because it will now be flavoured by the chorizo. Tip in the tomato and kale.
5 Remove the hot dish from the oven and tip in the remaining olive oil. Swill it around so that the whole dish is lightly coated in the oil.
6 Give the egg mix a final stir and tip everything into the hot dish. Place back in the oven and bake until the eggs are cooked — about 12-18 mins.
©www.eggrecipes.co.uk

10 Monday

11 Tuesday

12 Wednesday

13 Thursday

14 Friday

15 Saturday

16 Sunday

Blast from the past

This turn-table from the 1960s is still going strong

My much-loved record player

I still have the Bush record player that my husband bought for me on my 21st birthday in 1969. It works as well today. Before I retired I worked as an activities organiser in a nursing home and used to run regular reminiscence sessions with the residents and often took my trusty old record player to work. The residents would love to sing along with old favourites like Mrs Mills on her piano and Vera Lynn (a very popular and regular visitor to the home). Singing and listening to music was a great way to get them to open up and share their memories.

My favourite singers were Elvis Presley and Jim Reeves in the Sixties and Seventies. When my two children came along they enjoyed listening to Pinky and Perky and the Wombles. They loved taking it in turns to choose the next record to play. Now a doting grandma to Charlotte, aged eight, and Jersey, aged seven, I retrieved my record player out from under the bed recently where it had been languishing in recent years. They couldn't believe we had LPs and 45s and a machine like a record player just to listen to our favourite singers or music. I suppose looking at an MP3 player these days it is hard to imagine. As they also pointed out to me, the songs were much shorter then. At least we could dance to them energetically for a few minutes. These days one is exhausted halfway through!

Pam Simpson, Inverness

Quick brain boost

Can you solve this riddle?
Which clever invention allows you to see right through a wall?

Answer below

Garden inspiration

PIC SHUTTERSTOCK

Great garden tip

If you are leaving your allotment or vegetable bed to lie fallow after the produce has been harvested, save yourself further time and trouble by covering the whole area with old carpet. This suppresses the growth of weeds and cuts out the backbreaking task of digging it over. Wool and cotton carpets are suitable although they will eventually rot down; nylon carpets will last forever. Avoid using any carpets backed with rubber or latex. Make sure the carpet is weighted down so it doesn't blow away in the winter gales.

Senior moments

My husband had been to get his eyes tested and asked me to go along with him to the opticians to find some glasses. After trying on several pairs, he announced that he'd decided on a pair which felt comfortable. I thought they looked really familiar at which point I realised he was still wearing his old glasses.

Linda Grime, Oldham

What a good idea!

If you have trouble bending down, I've got a nifty solution for picking things up from the floor. I glued an old fridge magnet to the bottom of a walking stick, so that the magnetic side was facing down to the floor. Now I have no problem picking up small objects from the floor and especially pins when I am sewing.

Margaret Smith, County Durham

Quick brain boost answer: A window!

Recipe of the week

BRAMLEY APPLE & GINGER PIE

Serves: 4
Preparation time: 20–25 mins
Cooking time: 35 mins

1 packet of ready-made sweet pastry or shortcrust pastry
4 large Bramley apples, peeled, cored and roughly chopped
30g (1oz) butter, optional
2 thumb-sized pieces of fresh ginger, peeled and grated finely
6 balls of stem ginger, roughly chopped
Stem ginger syrup from jar
$^1/_2$ tbsp fresh lemon thyme leaves, finely chopped
3 egg yolks
1 whole egg
2 tsp fennel seeds
Golden caster sugar, optional

1 Preheat the oven to 220°C/ 425°F/ Gas Mark 7.
2. Put the apples in a pan with the stem ginger syrup, butter and thyme.
3 Grate the fresh ginger finely then squeeze all the juice into the pan and discard the pulp.
4 Bring the apples to a simmer and put a lid on the pan. Poach until tender. Remove the lid and rapidly simmer until all obvious wateriness has evaporated. Allow to cool, then beat in the egg yolks.
5 Stir in the stem ginger.
6 Lightly flour the work surface and then roll out the pastry only a little thicker than a £1 coin. Scatter the fennel seeds over the pastry and lightly roll them into it.
7 Cut a few long strips of pastry from around the outside and arrange them around the rim of a medium pie dish. Spoon the apple mixture into the dish and put a pie bird in the middle. Lay the pastry over the top making a small incision to let the bird's head through. Trim the sides and crimp the border and pastry lid together.
8 Brush with egg wash then scatter the caster sugar.
9 Bake for 25–35 mins.
© www.bramleyapples.co.uk

17 Monday

18 Tuesday

19 Wednesday

20 Thursday

21 Friday

22 Saturday

23 Sunday

Blast from the past

Yvonne with her mum, dad and brother John

Throughing the baby...

During the war our house in Kent was badly damaged by a V2 rocket. We were evacuated all the way to Tiree, an island on the Inner Hebrides as my dad was in the RAF and stationed there. I made friends with Margaret, one of the village children. Her Mammy had just had a new baby – or 'babby' as Margaret pronounced it. I had a china doll and Margaret and I washed her clothes and pegged them out to dry. As Margaret knew how to bath a 'babby' we decided to wash the doll. We drew water from the well, poured it into a bowl, then placed the 'babby' in the water. My job was to carefully hold her head out of the water. Margaret washed her, then carefully laid her on an old towel and dried her. We dressed her again, put her into the pram and took her for a walk. Afterwards I left the doll in the pram. Next day I went to pick her up and all I had in my hands was the body! I screamed and Mum explained that the doll's arms, legs and head moved by rubber bands inside the doll's body and the water had perished the band. "I can make new elastic bands for it," she smiled. With deft fingers and a crochet hook, Mum joined the doll together again. I explained to Margaret: "We must never bath the 'babby' again!" We were only four years old.

Yvonne Parsons, Devon

What a good idea!

When you're filling up the dishwasher at the end of the day, keep a section of the cutlery basket free and pop your dirty dish cloth in there. It will come out lovely and clean and save you washing it separately in the washing machine, where it might make your other laundry smell. So that's two household jobs done in one! **Suzanne Todd, County Tyrone**

Quick brain boost

What comes next in this number sequence?

87, 82, 77, 72, 67, 62, ??   Answer below

Garden inspiration

PIC: UNIVERSITY OF LIVERPOOL NESS BOTANIC GARDENS

Visit Ness Botanic Gardens

Now owned by the University of Liverpool, Ness Botanic Gardens were created over a century ago by cotton merchant and plant enthusiast Arthur Kilpin Bulley. Autumn is the perfect time to see the exquisite blue Gentiana sino-ornata, one of the many plants he introduced to this country. The berries on the national collection of Sorbus are another source of autumn colour as well as the acers in the woodland garden. A recent innovation is Wilder-Ness, an area that has been turned into a wildflower meadow overlooking the Dee estuary.
**Visit www.nessgardens.org.uk
or call 0845 0304063**

Senior moments

I needed some 2nd class stamps so I went into the Post Office to get some. When I got to the counter I said to the postmistress: "Please can I have 15 2nd hand stamps?" And then it dawned on me what I'd just said. Imagine my embarrassment! At least it gave everyone in the queue, including myself, a good laugh.
Grace Rayner, Burnley

Quick brain boost answer: **57** (the rule is: –5 each time)

Recipe of the week

WARM SMOKED MACKEREL & COLESLAW

Serves: 2
Preparation time: 10mins
Cooking time: 10 mins

3 heaped tbsp mayonnaise
3 heaped tbsp Greek yogurt
2 tsp Dijon mustard
1 tsp wholegrain mustard
1$^1/_2$ tsp white wine vinegar
200g (7oz) of raw white cabbage, very finely shredded
1$^1/_2$ tbsp dill fronds, roughly chopped
$^1/_2$ tbsp finely chopped chives
1 large Bramley apple, sliced thinly and cut into very fine strips
2 fillets of smoked mackerel, not peppered

1 Combine the mayonnaise and Greek yogurt with the mustards and vinegar.
2 Stir in the shredded cabbage and herbs then season with a little salt. Leave for 10–15 mins to soften.
3 Slice the apple very finely, then cut very thinly and stir through the coleslaw.
4 Warm the mackerel gently under the grill. Peel off the skin once removed from the oven.
5 Put a small mound of the coleslaw on each plate and arrange some warmed mackerel on top before serving.
© www.bramleyapples.co.uk

24 Monday

25 Tuesday

26 Wednesday

27 Thursday

28 Friday

29 Saturday

30 Sunday

Blast from the past

Gwen remembers going to school in a terraced house

The soldier I'll never forget

Another piece of my childhood was chipped away recently when a street of my wartime childhood was leveled ready for new build. It was a short street, tucked away and backing on to where I lived. I first went into one of its three-storey terraced houses in 1939. I was six, and lessons were organised in the front room until we could return to proper school. My best friend, Jean, lived in one of those houses and we lived in each other's pockets until we had to grow up. I remember the gas mantles were very fragile and any movement near them and poof... gone! So we had to be careful when we were being Ginger Rogers and Rita Hayworth.

My most abiding memory of the street is of a complete stranger, an ex-prisoner of war, returning home de-mobbed. A street party had been organised. Flags and 'welcome home' streamers were strung across the street. The crowd gathered but kept absolutely quiet until he rounded the corner and then everyone erupted with screams and flung themselves at him. He was transfixed, kitbag dropping off his shoulder, his greatcoat dangling from the other. The expression on his face is etched in my memory – a mixture of surprise, incomprehension and fear. I think he wanted to run away but he couldn't move. I realised for the first time that not all surprises are wonderful to receive. I felt sorry for that soldier in a moment which should have been joyous.

Gwen Collins, Lincs

Quick brain boost

Can you crack the code? **If N=T, M=S and L=R what does MNLUNYACYM say?** Answer below

Garden inspiration

PIC: ALAMY

Great garden tip

Use autumn garden waste to start a compost heap. Buy a bin or construct a partially enclosed area in which to put spent bedding and vegetable plants, grass cuttings, weeds (remove any tap roots from the weeds first) and shredded leaves. Never add any diseased material such as rose leaves affected by black spot. From the kitchen, add fruit and vegetable peelings as well as tea bags, coffee grounds and shredded paper. Turn the composting material over once a week to encourage it to rot down quickly.

Senior moments

My friends' mother was having trouble with her memory so she recently went to the doctors to have a test for dementia. Afterwards, she told us: "I thought doctors were supposed to be clever people, but Dr James has just asked me the name of the Prime Minister. I would have thought he'd be bright enough to have known that!"   **Mrs Eckhardt, Sheffield**

What a good idea!

Don't throw away old toilet roll tubes – they always come in for fun activities with the grandchildren. One way to use them is to make a bird feeder. To do this, warm up lard and some birdseed in a bowl and roll the toilet paper tubes in this mixture. Finally attach some garden string and hang them up in the bushes for the birds.   **J Bennett, Kent**

Quick brain boost answer: Strategies (each letter is shifted 7 letters down the alphabet)

Recipe of the week

BRUSCHETTA WITH ROAST SHALLOTS & BRIE

Serves: 4
Preparation time: 15 mins
Cooking time: 25-30 mins

12 shallots, peeled and cut in half
1 lemon, quartered
1 small bunch fresh thyme
2 tbsp extra virgin olive oil
200g (8oz) brie, sliced
1 garlic clove, cut in half and lightly bruised
4 slices thick-cut bread

1 Place the shallots in a roasting tin with the thyme scattered over. Squeeze the juice from the lemon quarters into the tin and add the skins. Add the extra virgin olive oil and toss to mix.

2 Roast in the oven at 180°C/350°F/Gas Mark 4 for about 15-20 mins until the shallots are soft and just beginning to caramelise.

3 Five mins before the shallots finish roasting, toast the bread on both sides under the grill and rub one side of each slice with the cut side of the bruised garlic.

4 When the shallots are done stir to coat in the pan juices, discard the lemon skins and any large, woody stalks of thyme.

5 Top each slice of bread with the lemony shallots, arrange the brie on top and return to the grill for a couple of mins until the cheese melts. Season to taste and serve with a fresh green salad.

©www.UKShallot.com

31 Monday

1 Tuesday

2 Wednesday

3 Thursday

4 Friday

5 Saturday

6 Sunday

Blast from the past

The fun of the fair

I have always loved funfairs and circuses and would go whenever possible in Maidenhead, where I lived. During the war, many staff were away fighting and fuel was almost impossible to get, but Beach's Fair made their base on Hines Meadow near Maidenhead and built the dodgems (sixpence a ride) and the Noah's Ark (threepence a ride) into an old Chipperfield's Circus tent with a kiddie ride and stalls inside which seemed to pass the blackout regulations. It certainly helped lift the gloom.

After the war I was a boarder at Newbury Grammar School and we were let out to go to the Newbury Michaelmas Fair. The equipment was still the same as that used pre-war and there were no new rides, so there would be up to five sets of dodgems and lots of wonderful side-shows. I remember Tommy 'Twinkle Toes' Jacobson who had no arms but did amazing things with his feet. A big attraction back then was Alf Weston's boxing booth (admission one shilling) where there was either a three-round or six-round bout. The fair boxers took on all-comers – and boxing in the three-round bout left them nicely warmed up for the six-round one! I got married in 1958 and, moved to Reading. I'm pleased to say that, as the owner of the first in-store bakery in Reading, I supplied hot-dog rolls and pies for many years to three generations of fair families and was proud to call them my friends.

John Spindler, Lancs

What a good idea!

I love making Yorkshire puddings, although I find they can be a bit messy to do. So, to make the process easier, pour the Yorkshire pudding mixture into bun tins from a clean teapot instead of from a jug. It pours much better this way and it means you don't splash mixture all over the rest of the tin.

Joan Jones, Hampshir

Quick brain boost

Recipe of the week

Garden inspiration

PIC: SHUTTERSTOCK

Jobs for November

◆ Give the lawn its final cut and apply fertiliser.
◆ Prune deciduous trees and shrubs. Once the leaves have fallen it is easier to see damaged, weak or lopsided growth that needs to be removed.
◆ Plant tulip bulbs.
◆ Place grease bands around fruit trees to protect them from winter moths.
◆ Mint roots can be dug up and put in pots for a winter supply.
◆ Pull up half-hardy vegetables such as runner beans and tomatoes. Healthy plants can be composted.
◆ Support sprouting broccoli and Brussels sprout plants with canes.

HALLOWE'EN CUPCAKES

Serves: 12
Preparation time: 10 mins
Cooking time: 25 mins

175g (6oz) Stork
175g (6oz) Golden caster sugar
300g (11oz) self-raising flour, sieved
3 medium eggs
5 tbsp milk
$\frac{1}{2}$ tsp baking powder
100g (4oz) cooked pumpkin or butternut squash, mashed
50g (2oz) chocolate and hazelnut spread
Zest of 1 orange
Topping:
115g (4oz) icing sugar
A little orange juice
55g (2oz) plain chocolate, melted or use chocolate and hazelnut spread
Liquorice sweets and laces to decorate

1 Preheat the oven to 200°C/400°F/Gas Mark 6. Then place the first six ingredients into a bowl, and beat with a wooden spoon until the mixture is smooth.
2 Stir in pumpkin mash and orange zest.
3 Divide half the mixture evenly between the 12 paper cases.
4 Add a $\frac{1}{2}$ tsp chocolate spread and then top with remaining mix. Bake in a preheated oven for 20-25 mins.
5 Add a little orange juice to the icing sugar until thick and spread over the muffins.
6 Pipe the melted chocolate in 4 circles over the top and then drag a skewer through to give the cobweb effect. Place the sweets and laces on top to look like a spider.
© www.bakewithstork.com

Senior moments

My son and I went to visit my husband in hospital where we found him asleep. As we sat down, I thought, 'Where did he get those pyjamas?' Suddenly, me and my son looked at each other and said: "That's not Dad." We were on the wrong ward! When we found my husband, I gave him a kiss and was glad I hadn't mistakenly woken up the lookalike that way.

Rachel Swinton, Newcastle

7 Monday

8 Tuesday

9 Wednesday

10 Thursday

11 Friday

12 Saturday

13 Sunday

Blast from the past

At eight weeks old Kim became a much-loved companion

My lovely dog, Kim

When I passed the 11-plus, I was promised a puppy. And to my great joy, we got Kim, at just eight weeks old. He was wonderful and became my best friend and constant companion. I had a bicycle – the old-fashioned, sit-up-and-beg type with my basket on the front. I used to love to go out on it with Kim in the basket.

As he got a bit older and wasn't such a puppy we also used to walk the mile and a half to Sidmouth beach. He would go a bit wild – sometimes running off with other people's towels and he loved to dash in and out of the sea. He would run so much he would tire himself out and I would end up carrying him home. He was a well-exercised dog, as not only did I take him for a walk every day after school, but my dad took him for long walks during the day – whatever the weather. He was well looked after – no tinned food for him, only fresh cooked meat and bones. Although that didn't stop him bringing home a smelly dead mole one day – ugh! He lived until he was 21 years old – and was great company for my father after my mother died. We were all so upset when he finally left us – leaving a great gap in our lives. **Mrs H Clapp, Devon**

What a good idea!

Did you know kiwi fruits are great at making your meat even more tender? Whenever I cook lamb chops for Sunday lunch, I always place several slices of kiwi fruit on top of the meat before I grill it. The meat comes out tasting deliciously soft and tender and there are always plenty of compliments forthcoming from around the dinner table.
Angela Codling, West Yorkshire

Quick brain boost

Can you solve this riddle?
**Take off my skin – I won't cry, but you will!
What am I?**
Answer below

Garden inspiration

PIC ALAMY

In bloom now: the last asters

Although asters are known as Michaelmas Daisies because they are in bloom on September 29 (St Michael's Day), they have a long flowering period and there are several varieties that are still brightening our gardens in November. The frikartii asters tend to be over earlier than this but Aster amellus 'King George' keeps its violet blue flowers until the first frosts. Asters come in white and many shades of pink as well as the sultry purples that go brilliantly with yellow rudbeckias such as R laciniata 'Autumn Sun'.

Senior moments

I was making a coffee when I found my milk was off. It wasn't past its sell-by-date so I decided to return it to the supermarket. Up I trotted to our local Tesco, where I asked the sales girl if I could have a refund. When she told me she couldn't help me, I irately said: "Why ever not?" She replied: "Because this milk is from Morrison's."

Mrs Hay, Warwickshire

Quick brain boost answer: An onion

Recipe of the week

CHICKEN & CHICKPEA CURRY

Serves: 4–6
Preparation time: 10 mins
Cooking time: 20 mins

1 onion, sliced
1 tbsp olive oil
1 clove garlic, finely chopped
2$\frac{1}{2}$cm (1in) root ginger peeled and grated
1 tsp turmeric
1 tsp curry powder
1 tbsp flour
4 chicken breasts, cut into chunks
400g can chickpeas, drained
$\frac{1}{2}$ chicken stock cube, dissolved in 300ml boiling water
100g (3$\frac{1}{2}$oz) spinach leaves
2 tbsps mango chutney
100ml (3$\frac{1}{2}$floz) natural low–fat yogurt
225g (8oz) basmati rice
1 tsp coriander seeds, toasted
25g (1oz) butter or spread
A handful of fresh coriander leaves, chopped

1 In a saucepan heat the olive oil over a moderate heat and fry the onion until soft. Then add the garlic, ginger, turmeric and curry powder and fry for 1 min.
2 Add the flour and cook for 1 min, then stir in the stock, stirring constantly. Add the chicken and simmer for 10 mins.
3 Meanwhile cook the rice according to pack instructions.
4 Add the chickpeas to the curry along with the spinach leaves and heat until the spinach leaves have just wilted. Then stir in the mango chutney and natural yogurt. Heat through gently, but be careful not to boil.
5 Drain the rice and stir in the spread, coriander seeds and the coriander leaves. Serve with the curry.

©www.floraproactiv.co.uk

14 Monday

15 Tuesday

16 Wednesday

17 Thursday

18 Friday

19 Saturday

20 Sunday

Blast from the past

Left, South Wales Nan, right, East London Nan

Those lethal home health cures

Before the NHS all our ailments were treated with home remedies and my two nans had a cure for everything. It appeared that the stronger smelling and the more evil tasting the remedy the more effective they believed it to be. Sometimes I had severe joint pains and my mother treated these with a kaolin poultice – a gooey cement-like paste heated and sandwiched between two pieces of gauze and applied to the aching limb. Getting the right temperature was a bit hit and miss and you risked having the skin burned off you in the process! My feet were a painful mass of chilblains, not helped by sleeping every night in the air raid shelter. Various remedies were tried to no effect. I was in agony until my Nan told me to, "Do a wee in that potty and soak your feet in it."

My grandfather wore a strip of bright pink thermogene cotton wool next to his skin to ward off chest infections. One day I pulled a piece from the drawer and held it to my face – agony! My eyes watered, I couldn't get my breath and I thought I would never breathe or see again. Camphorated oil was heated on the hob and rubbed in for our chest colds. We were dosed with cod liver oil and malt to promote growth and keep us healthy. I don't know if there was any value in these cures and remedies, but we survived. **Gwyneth Lowe, Essex**

What a good idea!

The kitchen bin quickly gets smelly but you can deodorise it easily just by sprinkling a layer of clean cat litter in the bottom of it. This not only gets rid of any smells – it also absorbs any liquids that spill into the bottom of the bin. This means you don't have to deal with a soggy bin bag when you take the rubbish out.

Sylvia Lees, Ken

Quick brain boost

What comes next in this number sequence?

30, 37, 31, 36, 32, 35, ??

Answer below

Garden inspiration

Great garden tip

Raking up leaves is one way of keeping warm on a chilly day but you can make the task easier by chopping them up first. Set the blades of the mower high and drive over the fallen leaves on your lawn. The shredded leaves can then be used as an organic mulch. Spread this up to five inches deep on flower borders and the vegetable patch, taking care that it doesn't touch the stems of plants. As they rot down, the leaves will release valuable nutrients into the soil.

Senior moments

When I went to see my 89-year-old mum, she told me that my brother had been to visit her the day before. She said that my brother had a bad back, but that it was getting much better now he'd been to see a psychopath. Imagine my relief when she realised that she'd meant to say osteopath.

Trevor Moore, Wakefield

Quick brain boost answer: **33** (the rule is: +7, -6, +5, -4, +3 etc)

Recipe of the week

ROLLED SHOULDER OF LAMB

Serves: 6-8
Preparation time: 25 mins
Cooking time: Medium: 25 mins per
1lb plus 25 minutes
Well done: 30 mins per 1lb plus 30 minutes

1.3kg (3lb) lean boned and rolled lamb shoulder joint
Salt and freshly milled black pepper
4tbsp fresh thyme leaves
Grated zest of 2 lemons
1 tbsp olive oil
For stuffing:
$1/2$ x 250g (8oz) pack prepared pilau rice
25g (1oz) fresh kale, rinsed and finely chopped
25g (1oz) sultanas
25g (1oz) toasted pine nuts

1 Preheat the oven to 180°C/350°F/Gas Mark 4.
2 Scatter half the thyme and half the lemon zest on a large tray. Unroll the joint (reserving any elasticated meat bands) and coat each side with the rosemary. Leave skin-side down and season.
3 To prepare stuffing; in a small bowl mix half the pilau rice with the remaining thyme, lemon and other stuffing ingredients, mix well and spread evenly over the lamb. Roll up and secure with butcher's string or elasticated meat bands. Weigh the joint and calculate the cooking time.
4 Place on a metal rack in a large non-stick roasting tin, drizzle with oil and roast in a preheated oven for the preferred cooking time.
5 Remove the joint from the oven, transfer to a large plate, cover and leave to rest for 15-20 mins.
6. Serve with vegetables and gravy.
© www.simplybeefandlamb.co.uk

21 Monday

22 Tuesday

23 Wednesday

24 Thursday

25 Friday

26 Saturday

27 Sunday

Blast from the past

Joyce's prompt action became the talk of the playground

Goosey, goosey gander...

I always loved being with my dad, especially when he was seeing to the geese. I loved the goslings and once I kept one as a pet and called him Billy. He often followed me to school but I had to bring him home again as he disrupted the other children. My dad had always said to me: "Don't go near a gander if a goose is sitting on eggs. They can be very dangerous."

One day when I was ten years old, our class was going to the recreation field. The footpath ran alongside our grounds, so on the way back my teacher said I could go on home. Off I went across the paddock, waving to my friends. Suddenly rushing towards me, wings outstretched, was the gander. I stood terrified, he looked so big. Then all at once Dad's words came back to me. I grabbed him by the neck, swung him around my head three times, let him go and ran for the gate. I was very shaken but all right. Next day at school I was the talk of the class, even the teacher was impressed. So was my dad.

Joyce Clifford, Herefordshire

What a good idea!

Estimated bills for my gas and electric are always such a pain. So when I know that the meter is due for reading, I take a photo of the meter, print it off and pop this in the window of my front door. When the meter reader comes, they can see exactly what my reading is even if I'm out.

A Clark, County Durham

Quick brain boost

Can you crack the code? **If I=A, M=E and Z=R what does ZMDMITQVO say?**
Answer below

Garden inspiration

PIC: LEE BEE

Visit Harlow Carr Gardens

As you would expect from a garden owned by the Royal Horticultural Society, the 58 acres of Harlow Carr in Yorkshire offers something for everyone. Its varied landscapes include woodland, perennial borders, wildflower meadows and the longest streamside garden in the country. In autumn the recently expanded winter walk comes into its own with vibrant dogwoods and the blue stem willow (Salix irrorata). For keen gardeners, workshops and courses are run throughout the year. On a chilly day, Betty's tearoom provides a welcome retreat for all visitors.

Senior moments

My friend had just had a new grandson and so I decided to knit a cardigan for the baby. About half way through knitting, I was flabbergasted by just how much yarn I'd used. It wasn't until I joined all the separate pieces together that I realised the reason I'd gone through so much yarn was because I'd knitted three sleeves.

Christine Wilbraham, Chester

Quick brain boost answer: Revealing (each letter is shifted 8 letters up the alphabet)

Recipe of the week

LAMB TAGINE

Serves: 4
Preparation time: 20 mins
Cooking time: 90 mins

450g (1lb) lean diced lamb
1 tsp ground black pepper
3 tsp paprika
1 tsp ground cinnamon
2 tsp turmeric
1 tbsp Flora Cuisine
1 large onion
1 clove garlic
55g (2oz) dried apricots
25g (1oz) sultanas or raisins
25g (1oz) toasted flaked almonds
2 tsp honey
570ml (1pt) lamb stock
2 x 400g (14oz) tinned chopped tomatoes
2 tsp tomato purée
1 tbsp fresh coriander chopped, to garnish
1 tbsp fresh parsley chopped, to garnish

1 Preheat oven to 170°C/325°F/Gas Mark 3.
2 Toss the lamb with black pepper, paprika, cinnamon and turmeric, coating evenly.
3 Heat Flora Cuisine in a casserole dish, add in onion and garlic and fry until softened.
4 Add spiced lamb and fry until the meat is browned, around 5 minutes, stirring now and then.
5 Add in the remaining ingredients, mix well and bring to the boil.
6 Cover and transfer to the oven and cook for 1 hour 30 mins. Garnish with the fresh coriander and parsley and serve with rice.
© www.flora.com

28 Monday

29 Tuesday

30 Wednesday

1 Thursday

2 Friday

3 Saturday

4 Sunday

Blast from the past

Joan, aged 15 in 1958.

My naughty older brother

I bought my first pair of high heels when I was 16 in 1959. I thought they were wonderful. They were black suedette peep-toes with a diamante ring about the size of the old halfpenny on the front of the shoe near the open toe. They cost me £1 19s 11d in old money. I could walk in them very well – that wasn't the problem. One evening I was going out with the girls and I went into the cupboard to get my shoes out. I noticed that one of the diamante rings was missing. I searched the cupboard and all over the house for it in case it had fallen off, but no luck. I later discovered that my 'clever' older brother had stolen it and made a brooch with it to give to his girlfriend. I was so angry and upset. I pulled the ring off the other shoe and threw it at him. We argued and I cried and I didn't speak to him for two weeks. We're okay now though – and sometimes the incident gets mentioned with a laugh or two. Oh yes, and I still went out that night, minus the diamante rings.

Joan Mee, Doncaster

What a good idea!

I always find black clothes a real nuisance for collecting fluff from my scarf, my rug, anything. But I have found that winding a strip of builder's gaffer tape around the palm of my hand to brush over the fabric works a treat for getting rid of the fluff. It's a lot cheaper than buying lots of lint rollers.

Kathleen Bentley, West Yorkshire

Quick brain boost

Garden inspiration

PIC ALAMY

Jobs for December

◆ Protect pots from frost by wrapping them in bubble wrap. Also outside taps.
◆ Book your lawnmower in for a service.
◆ Clear fallen leaves away from alpine plants as they will die if left damp. Spread alpine grit around the plants to encourage regrowth.
◆ Aerate any badly-drained areas of lawn on a mild day.
◆ Prune sambucus for summer foliage.
◆ Roses can still be planted in mild weather.
◆ Float rubber balls on the pond to prevent a thick layer of ice forming.
◆ When potted bulbs have two-inch shoots, bring indoors to a cool room. Keep watered.

Senior moments

A friend recently went Christmas shopping and going into a book store, she asked a member of staff: "Excuse me, please can you tell me where the hysterical section is?" She, of course, meant the historical section. She said she'd been watching a catch-up version of Coronation Street which she blames for her blunder. It certainly gave her and the staff a chuckle.

Mrs D Brookfield, Sheffield

Recipe of the week

APRICOT & STILTON CANAPÉS

Makes: 45
Preparation time: 15 mins
Cooking time: 15 mins

1 sheet of ready-rolled puff pastry
1 medium egg beaten
135g (4¹/₂oz) Stilton cheese
12 tsp apricot jam
25g (1oz) chopped walnuts

1 Preheat the oven to 200°C/400°F/ Gas Mark 6.
2 Using a pastry cutter, cut bite-sized disks (4cm wide) from the pastry and lay them on to a greased baking tray
3 Pierce each disk a few times using a fork and brush with a little beaten egg. Top each with a slice of Stilton, pressing it down in the middle a little. Cook in the oven for 10 minutes.
4 Take out of the oven and add about ¹/₄tsp of apricot jam to each canapé and a piece of chopped walnut. Return to the oven for 5minutes until they're browned.
5 Allow to cool for a few minutes and serve warm or cold.

©www.streamlinefoods.co.uk

5 Monday

6 Tuesday

7 Wednesday

8 Thursday

9 Friday

10 Saturday

11 Sunday

Blast from the past

Laura (centre) was a bit too enthralled by a Disney film

Is that the time?

I remember queuing for hours one Saturday afternoon when I was about ten, together with my two cousins, to see Snow White and the Seven Dwarfs. We sat patiently through the uninteresting B film first before Snow White started. We were so entranced with this magical film that we decided to stay on and see it through again, so once more we impatiently watched the B film through and just at the vital part of Snow White, we were amazed to see my mother at the end of the row with a couple of usherettes, shining their torches on us.

"Quick Mom," I shouted, "there's a seat by me." Apparently, by 7pm my parents were worried sick wondering what could have happened to us as we had left home about 1pm, so they had each gone a different route to the cinema hoping to find us. After being assured by the manager that all the children had left at the end of the matinee performance, they were escorted through a very annoyed audience to check that we were not still there! When they did find us, we were assured that Snow White's misfortunes would be nothing compared to those awaiting us when we got home!

Laura Rosier, Worcester

What a good idea!

Recipes often tell you to add some grated orange peel to add some extra flavour. But grating an orange can be quite difficult to do, especially if you don't have very strong hands. So before you get the grater out, put the orange in the freezer for an hour. This makes the fruit firmer and it becomes much easier to grate and peel.

Jessica Lindfield, London

Quick brain boost

Can you solve this riddle?

Forward I am heavy, but backward I am not. What am I?

Answer below

Garden inspiration

PIC: SHUTTERSTOCK

In bloom now: indoor bulbs

Nothing cheers up a grey December day as certainly as a bowl of Hyacinth 'White Pearl' or paper white narcissi filling the room with their delicate perfume. To have them in bloom for the festive season requires some forward planning as the prepared bulbs should be planted at the end of September or beginning of October. They then need to be kept in a cool (9°C/48°F) dark place for 12-15 weeks before being brought into the house. Push small twiggy branches into the compost to prop up top-heavy flowers.

Senior moments

I rather fancied some sherry so I went to my local supermarket to buy a bottle. When I got to the counter, I asked the young man if I could please have a bottle of armadillo. He looked blank and said they did not sell that here. I went home and suddenly remembered that I'd meant amontillado sherry – not armadillo.

Dorothy Cooper, Kent

Quick brain boost answer: Ton

Recipe of the week

BAKED BRAMLEY APPLES

Serves: 4
Preparation time: 10 mins
Cooking time: 20 mins

100g (4oz) butter, room temperature
2 tbsp walnuts, broken
4 oatcakes, coarsely broken
4 Medjool dates, stoned and roughly chopped
2 tbsp honey
2 Muscovado sugar
1/2 tsp coarse ground black pepper
Good pinch of cloves, ground
A grating of nutmeg
4 medium Bramley apples
4 bay leaves
Clotted cream to serve, optional

1 Preheat the oven to 220°C/ 425°F/ Gas Mark 7.
2 Mix everything but the bay and apples in a mixing bowl, thoroughly combining it all together.
3 Core the apples, then using a knife, widen the tunnel and cut more of a funnel shape in the top half of the hole in order to accommodate the filling. Make a slit, just through the skin around the middle or equator of the apple.
4 Lay each apple in a baking tray each on top of a small square of baking paper.
5 Stuff each apple well and insert a bay leaf lengthways down between the stuffing and the flesh of the apple.
6 Bake for 20 mins or until the apple is totally soft and the slit has widened to reveal fluffy flesh.
7 If the stuffing appears to be burning on top simply press another little square of baking paper on top.
8 Serve with a dollop of clotted cream, if desired.
© www.bramleyapples.co.uk

12	Monday
13	Tuesday
14	Wednesday
15	Thursday
16	Friday
17	Saturday
18	Sunday

Blast from the past

A Christmas party in the pub was enjoyed by local children

Party at the pub

My friend Helen's parents kept a pub called the West End in Wolverhampton Street in Dudley back in the Fifties. The pub is no longer standing now, but back then every Christmas they would put on a party for all the children living around the neighbourhood. There would be lovely food, games and a visit from Santa Claus, which we all looked forward to. Helen's parents are not alive now but I always remember them for their generosity in times when people had not got a lot of money. This photograph brings it all back – that's Helen and I in the back row on the right wearing party hats. We remained friends throughout our schooldays and when it came time to leave we both went on to do a two-year hairdressing course at Dudley Technical College to gain our City and Guilds – which I'm pleased to say we did. Even after we met our future partners in the Sixties we still met at weekends and went dancing at the Queen's ballroom in Wolverhampton. Happy Days!

Catherine Grove, W Mids

What a good idea!

To apply marzipan to your Christmas cake, roll it out on to a piece of greaseproof paper sprinkled with icing sugar. Place the finished and cooled cake upside down on top of it, then slide your hand underneath the paper. Turn it the right way up and peel off the greaseproof paper and the marzipan will be still intact.

Jane Dagg, Bristol

Quick brain boost

What comes next in this number sequence?

5, 8, 7, 10, 9, 12, ??

Answer below

Recipe of the week

Garden inspiration

PIC: ALAMY

Great garden tip

Christmas cactus (Schlumbergera x buckleyi) will drop its flowers in protest if it is moved and also prefers to be kept facing the same way. Make a small mark on the front of the pot to ensure it is always replaced correctly on a shelf or windowsill. To improve flowering, this houseplant can be put outside in the summer months after all danger of frost is over. It will only require watering if there is an exceptionally dry spell before it is brought indoors again in the autumn.

MINCE TARTS

Makes: 32
Preparation time: 20 mins
Cooking time: 15 mins

225g (8oz) plain flour
Pinch of salt
110g (4oz) butter or margarine, cut into small cubes
Low-calorie cooking spray
16 level tbsp mincemeat

1 Sift the flour and salt into a mixing bowl, reserving 1 tsp of the flour for dusting, then add the butter or margarine and gently rub it in with your fingertips. Add cold water until the mixture is wet enough to mix into a ball that leaves the sides of the bowl clean. Chill for 30 mins.
2 Preheat the oven to 190°C/375°F/Gas Mark 5 and lightly spray 32 bun tin holes with low-calorie cooking spray.
3 Sprinkle the reserved flour over a work surface then roll out the pastry thinly. Cut out 32 rounds with a 7.5cm (3in) fluted cutter and use to line the bun tin holes.
4 Divide the mincemeat between the pastry cases, using about half a tablespoon for each one.
5 Roll out the remaining pastry trimmings and make some little stars with a cutter. Use these to decorate the tops of the tarts.
6 Bake for 15 mins or until the pastry is crisp and lightly coloured, then leave to cool on a wire rack.
7 Dust with a light sprinkling of icing sugar if desired.
©Slimming World

Senior moments

It was Christmas Eve and I just had the last few parcels to wrap when I realised that my mobile phone was missing. So I phoned my number from the landline to see if I could find where it was. I, of course, eventually traced it back to one of the presents, where it was wrapped up in my grandson's snuggle blanket.

Penny Taylor, Dorchester, Dorset

Quick brain boost answer: **11** (the rule is: +3,-1,+3,-1 etc)

19 Monday

20 Tuesday

21 Wednesday

22 Thursday

23 Friday

24 Saturday

25 Sunday

Blast from the past

Pat's curls were cut off when she had a scarlet fever rash

Christmas in hospital

In December 1938, when I was three, I was taken very ill with diphtheria and scarlet fever (together!) and clearly remember being wrapped in a blanket and carried out of the house and into a cream-coloured ambulance. Arriving at the hospital I was put in a room on my own and there were several doctors and nurses around my bed. When my parents arrived to see me, my mum looked very sad as all my curly hair had been cut off as the scarlet fever rash was all over my head and body.

When I got better I was moved to a children's ward – this to me was great fun being with lots of girls and boys. As it was nearly Christmas there were lots of decorations and a big Christmas tree stood in the middle of the ward. One evening when we were all in bed, Father Christmas arrived. Such excitement! I was given a model of Popeye the Sailor Man and when you took off his sailor's hat you found he was full of sweets. I've always looked back on this hospital episode as quite an adventure and only found out years later that I was very close to losing my life the night I arrived at the hospital.

Pat Rose, Sidmouth, Devon

What a good idea!

Save money on your gas and electricity by turning down the temperature on your oven for the last five or ten minutes of cooking. Your oven will keep warm enough to finish off heating your food through properly, but you should notice that your bills start to go down slightly each month.

David Jackson, Lancashire

Quick brain boost

Can you crack the code? **If G=N, 5=I and 3=E what does 3GF54DJ3G3B say?** Answer below

Recipe of the week

SNOWMAN CUPCAKES

Serves: 12
Preparation time: 15 mins
Cooking time: 20 mins

For the cakes:
115g (4oz) spreadable butter or margarine
115g (4oz) caster sugar
2 eggs, medium
115g (4oz) self-raising flour
25g (1oz) cocoa powder, mixed with 1 tbsp water
For the icing:
55g (2oz) spreadable butter or margarine
225g icing sugar, sieved
1 tbsp milk
55g (2oz) white chocolate, melted
Decoration:
55g (2oz) desiccated coconut
Orange cake decorations or coloured fondant for nose
Chocolate buttons for hat
Chocolate drops for eyes

1 Preheat oven to 180°C/350°F/Gas Mark 4.
2 Weigh your eggs. Note the weight and measure the same amount of butter, sugar and flour.
3 Place all the ingredients in a mixing bowl and beat with a wooden spoon 2-3 mins until well mixed. Place dessertspoons of the mixture in 10-12 paper cases or greased bun tins. Bake for around 20 mins until soft and springy to touch. Cool on a wire tray.
4 Mix icing ingredients together and spread over the cakes. Sprinkle with coconut and decorate as a snowman face using the buttons cut in half for the hat, the chocolate drops for eyes and orange decoration for nose.
© www.flora.com

Garden inspiration

PIC: CHARLIE HOPKINSON

Visit Chelsea Physic Garden

Open all year round, the walled Chelsea Physic Garden was founded in 1673 by the Worshipful Society of Apothecaries. Its purpose was the study of the medicinal qualities of plants. A position near the Thames was chosen to allow non-native plants to grow in a warmer micro-climate and, as proof of this, the garden has the largest outdoor fruiting olive tree in Britain. It also features an ancient rock garden that is Grade II listed. In December every year, the garden hosts a popular Christmas fair. Visit www.chelseaphysicgarden.co.uk or call 0207 352 5646

Senior moments

I was watching a TV quiz show with my husband, when one of the questions that came up was, 'Who did John Lennon marry in 1969?' Quick as a flash I shouted out: "Orinoco!" Orinoco is of course one of the Wombles. I'd actually meant to say Yoko Ono, but my husband will never let me live this one down now.

Beryl Smith, Manchester

Quick brain boost answer: Enlightened (number alternate letters and fill the alphabet in between eg A=1, B=A, C=2, D=B)

26 Monday

27 Tuesday

28 Wednesday

29 Thursday

30 Friday

31 Saturday

1 Sunday

Blast from the past

Hazel always remembers one special Christmas present

Precious Christmas gift

My dad was a fisherman on the Grimsby docks – which when he was working there after the war was a large and busy fishing port. He was away for three weeks at a time, then home for just two days. At Christmas it seemed to me that he was never at home. But I do remember one special time. I was nine years old and on Christmas morning there were my presents. There weren't many but to me they seemed a lot and I was excited as I opened them. The last one was the best – it was a bible and inside it was a note from Dad. It said:

> This little gift we've bought for you
> Just to prove our love is true
> So think of me while I'm away
> And all the best for Christmas Day

My first thought was, 'How did Father Christmas find Dad's ship?' I was sure Santa had gone to the ship to bring back it back for me. Of course, as the years went past I realised that Mam had put it there with the other presents. I still have the bible with its note inside and would not part with it. I loved my dad and miss him.

Hazel Atkinson, Lincs

What a good idea!

Limescale quickly builds up on the bottom of taps, but it's actually really easy to get rid of. Just cut a lemon in half and then fasten it, pulp side up, to the bottom of the tap with an elastic band. Leave it there overnight and then unfasten, give your tap a wipe and the lime scale should be gone.

Mrs D Wardle, Bristol

Quick brain boost

Can you unscramble this anagram to make an 11-letter word?

BARKS DEBATE

Answer below

Garden inspiration

PIC-ALAMY

In bloom now: Christmas rose

In a sheltered spot, you might find a Christmas rose (Helleborus niger) in bloom on December 25, but these hardy plants really come into their own from mid-winter onwards. The original pure white form has been hybridised to give us a much wider choice of colours including pink, yellow, mauve and purple as well as speckled flowers. It is a good idea to cut away the large leaves so the blooms can be seen to better advantage. For an indoor display, float the flower heads in a shallow bowl of water.

Senior moments

Recently, a cash machine kept rejecting my card and I just couldn't understand why – it had always worked fine before. So when the machine spat out my card for the fourth time I took a closer look, only to realise that I had been trying to withdraw money from my bus pass. In my defence, they are a similar colour!

June Lomax, Huddersfield

Quick brain boost answer: Breadbasket

Recipe of the week

TURKEY ESCALOPES

Serves: 4
Prep time: 10 mins
Cooking time: 10 mins

50g (2oz) plain flour
Salt and pepper
2 eggs, beaten
150g (5oz) dry breadcrumbs
25g (1oz) Parmesan cheese, finely grated
4 quick cook British turkey steaks
4 tbsp tomato purée
4 tbsp oil

1 Put the flour in a large shallow bowl or plate and season with plenty of salt and pepper.
2 Put the beaten eggs in another shallow dish, and leave to one side. Mix the breadcrumbs and Parmesan on another large plate.
3 Take a turkey steak and spread one side with a tablespoon of tomato purée. Place it in the dish of seasoned flour, turning so both sides of the steak are coated.
4 Dip the steak in the beaten egg, turning so both sides are coated, then shake off the excess.
5 Place the steak in the breadcrumb mix, pressing it in well so it is covered on both sides.
6 Repeat with the remaining steaks.
7 To cook, heat a large frying pan and add 2 tbsp oil. When hot add two turkey steaks, and fry for 3–4mins on each side until crisp and golden. Cook in batches of two.

© www.britishturkey.co.uk

2017 year planner

	JANUARY	FEBRUARY	MARCH	APRIL	MAY	JUNE
MON					1	
TUES					2	
WED		1	1		3	
THUR		2	2		4	1
FRI		3	3		5	2
SAT		4	4	1	6	3
SUN	1	5	5	2	7	4
MON	2	6	6	3	8	5
TUES	3	7	7	4	9	6
WED	4	8	8	5	10	7
THUR	5	9	9	6	11	8
FRI	6	10	10	7	12	9
SAT	7	11	11	8	13	10
SUN	8	12	12	9	14	11
MON	9	13	13	10	15	12
TUES	10	14	14	11	16	13
WED	11	15	15	12	17	14
THUR	12	16	16	13	18	15
FRI	13	17	17	14	19	16
SAT	14	18	18	15	20	17
SUN	15	19	19	16	21	18
MON	16	20	20	17	22	19
TUES	17	21	21	18	23	20
WED	18	22	22	19	24	21
THUR	19	23	23	20	25	22
FRI	20	24	24	21	26	23
SAT	21	25	25	22	27	24
SUN	22	26	26	23	28	25
MON	23	27	27	24	29	26
TUES	24	28	28	25	30	27
WED	25		29	26	31	28
THUR	26		30	27		29
FRI	27		31	28		30
SAT	28			29		
SUN	29			30		
MON	30					
TUES	31					
WED						

						MON
	1					TUES
	2			1		WED
	3			2		THUR
	4	1		3	1	FRI
1	5	2		4	2	SAT
2	6	3	1	5	3	SUN
3	7	4	2	6	4	MON
4	8	5	3	7	5	TUES
5	9	6	4	8	6	WED
6	10	7	5	9	7	THUR
7	11	8	6	10	8	FRI
8	12	9	7	11	9	SAT
9	13	10	8	12	10	SUN
10	14	11	9	13	11	MON
11	15	12	10	14	12	TUES
12	16	13	11	15	13	WED
13	17	14	12	16	14	THUR
14	18	15	13	17	15	FRI
15	19	16	14	18	16	SAT
16	20	17	15	19	17	SUN
17	21	§8	16	20	18	MON
18	22	19	17	21	19	TUES
19	23	20	18	22	20	WED
20	24	21	19	23	21	THUR
21	25	22	20	24	22	FRI
22	26	23	21	25	23	SAT
23	27	24	22	26	24	SUN
24	28	25	23	27	25	MON
25	29	26	24	28	26	TUES
26	30	27	25	29	27	WED
27	31	28	26	30	28	THUR
28		29	27		29	FRI
29		30	28		30	SAT
30			29		31	SUN
31			30			MON
			31			TUES
						WED

Quiz answers

How did you do with the quiz questions on pages 32–37?

Phrase & Fable Quiz
(pages 32 and 33)

1 B) Mine coal
2 A) 1992
3 B) Reversing of the natural order of things
4 A) Pig Latin
5 C) Knobstick Wedding
6 C) William Tell
7 C) Nudge nudge, wink wink
8 C) As daft as a brush
9 B) Ealing comedies
10 C) Frequently asked questions
11 C) The Four Horsemen of the Apocalypse
12 A) Resolved
13 B) Horseshoes
14 A) Flew too close to the sun
15 B) Disclosed a secret
16 A) Manna
17 B) Waitresses
18 B) Odette
19 C) Pandora's
20 B) Pontefract Cakes
21 B) Halcyon days
22 A) Quartermaster
23 C) Received Pronunciation
24 C) The Joneses
25 A) A betrayal
26 A) Free
27 A) Grog

Inventions Quiz
(pages 34 and 35)

1 C) Electric lighting
2 A) Washing machines
3 A) Sticky tape
4 B) The World Wide Web
5 C) Microwave
6 A) Dishwasher
7 B) ZX Spectrum
8 B) 22°C
9 C) Brownie
10 A) iPad
11 B) Airfryer
12 A) Blu-Tack
13 C) e-Readers
14 A) 1970s
15 C) Ballpoint Pen
16 B) Cars
17 A) Calculators
18 C) Typewriters
19 B) It was splinter-free
20 A) Tumble dryer
21 C) Hair straighteners
22 C) Hoover
23 A) Wimbledon
24 A) Mallard
25 A) Sewing machines

History Quiz
(pages 36 and 37)

1 A) 1066
2 B) Cambridge
3 A) Bannockburn
4 C) The Hundred Years' War
5 B) Canterbury Tales
6 B) The Welsh revolt
7 C) St Andrews
8 B) He was less than a year old at the time
9 A) Published a printed book
10 A) Bosworth
11 A) Annul his marriage
12 B) Peterborough
13 C) Jane Seymour
14 A) England and France
15 B) 1605
16 C) Samuel Pepys
17 A) Sir Robert Walpole
18 C) Great Yarmouth
19 B) The Times
20 B) Robert Peel
21 B) One penny
22 C) Britain's first symphony orchestra
23 C) Elizabeth Gaskell
24 A) Bank Holiday Act
25 B) Children under ten
26 A) 1881
27 A) Frank Matcham
28 C) 888, 246

RELAX & UNWIND

Homecoming

BY: MADDIE PURSLOW

How will Christina's father react to her big news?

Christina was on the last leg of her journey to Cumbria. Ahead of her the peaks rose up in sharp relief against the bright sky. As she crested the hill she had a clear view of her childhood home, Grizedale Farm. The roof was covered in frost and blue smoke rose from the chimney.

She pulled into the yard in time to see her father's bulky figure going into one of the sheds. He was dressed in his usual old jeans and ragged jumper. He'd known that she was coming home today but Christina guessed there would be no special treatment, the farm work went on as normal.

As she got out of the car, she called to him and he raised a hand in greeting. The back door juddered as she pushed it open. The kitchen was in darkness but the warmth from the stove made it more inviting. On the table, her father's newspaper was spread out next to an empty mug.

He followed her in. "All right?" he said. "Got here in good time then?"

Christina nodded.

"Help yourself to a brew. I'm waiting for the vet to come so I'll have to get on. Mrs Stebbings will be here later but I'm sure you can occupy yourself until then." And with that he was gone.

Christina had spent much of her childhood 'occupying herself' when she wasn't at boarding school. She dropped her handbag on to the rocking chair and went out to get her case. "Welcome home, Christina," she said.

At midday it was her father's custom to stop for coffee. When he found her in the kitchen, he looked as though he'd almost forgotten she was there. She poured them both a cup. The familiar farmyard smell mingling with the aroma of coffee took her back to the day that he had explained to her that her mother 'would never be coming back' and they would have to be brave and help each other as best they could.

Now they sat silently, each lost in their own thoughts. "Well, must get on!" her father said, abruptly rising to his feet.

"Wait, Dad! Don't you want to know why I'm here?"

He paused. "Just a visit, isn't it?"

"I've come to tell you Paul and I are getting married. He wanted to come with me, but couldn't get time off."

Christina waited for his reaction.

"Well," he said, resting his raw red hands on his hips. "Good. Good for you. But you needn't have come all this way to tell me. An invitation would have done. Now, I'll see if the vet's done with them ewes."

He stomped out, leaving Christina to finish her coffee. "An invitation would have done?" she repeated incredulously. Why weren't they able to talk to each other like any other father and daughter?

An hour later, Mrs Stebbings came bustling in, bringing with her the clean lavender smell that Christina remembered well. Ruth Stebbings had been coming to the farm every day since her mother died and was almost one of the family. She tidied up, made their evening meals and added a little femininity to the masculine routine of farm life.

She exclaimed: "Christina! What a lovely surprise! Does your dad know you're here?"

"He knows," she answered glumly.

"Are you here for long? Has Paul come as well?"

She fired questions as she moved around the cluttered kitchen. Her genuine interest moved Christina. Mrs Stebbings seemed more pleased to see her than her father was.

Seeing her sad expression, she asked: "Oh now, what's the matter?"

"I came to tell Dad we're getting married, and do you know what he said? He said I should have just sent him an invitation!"

Mrs Stebbings winced in sympathy and said: "Oh, Phil James, you really are a lost cause!"

"Lost cause? I often think he's not bothered about me at all."

"Oh, don't say that, love."

"Isn't that why he sent me away to school?"

'Lost cause? I often think he's not bothered about me at all'

ILLUSTRATION: KATE DAVIES

'He calls this his memory bank, but don't you ever tell him you've seen it'

"No, he thought he was doing the right thing so you'd have other girls around you. And he had to keep the farm going. He does care."

"Well, he's got a funny way of showing it."

Suddenly Mrs Stebbings rose to her feet. "What he said about the invitation – don't take that the wrong way. Let me show you something."

Going across to the oak dresser, she eased open a drawer and pulled out a tattered carrier bag. "He calls this his memory bank, but don't you ever tell him you've seen it."

She tipped the contents on to the table. There were birthday cards, photographs, school reports, programmes for school plays, everything that Christina had ever been involved in.

Mrs Stebbings went on: "He has never parted with anything to do with you. He just doesn't know how to express his feelings. He wanted the invitation to put in here. Something to keep."

Staring in amazement at the pile of mementoes, Christina tearfully resolved to tell her father all about her wedding plans whether he appeared interested or not. And, above all, she would make sure he had a special invitation to keep in his memory bank.

We had stars in our eyes: THE POSTER BOYS

A Matter of Life and Death had David Niven's character standing before a heavenly judge and jury

Handsome, suave and sophisticated, the 'idols of the Odeon' set hearts fluttering with dreams of being whirled elegantly around a dance floor or being kissed tenderly while a nightingale sang in Berkeley Square. The epitome of the debonair matinée idol was Michael Wilding who wooed and won Anna Neagle in such delightfully light-hearted films as Maytime in Mayfair and Spring in Park Lane. After the sombre war years, audiences were more than ready to be transported to a world in which men looked dashing in white tie and tails, ladies wore the latest Paris fashions and naturally everyone had a butler to answer the door, my dear.

There surely wasn't a female filmgoer who wasn't madly envious of the lucky girl who won David Niven in The Love Lottery, a film in which he is a famous movie star who finds himself offered as the prize in an international gambling venture. After returning from Hollywood to 'do his bit' as an officer in Rifle Brigade (where his batman was a young Peter Ustinov), Niven appeared in a number of war-based films, most memorably as the fatally injured RAF pilot Peter Carter in the Powell and Pressburger film, A Matter of Life and Death. Whichever role he played, Niven imbued it with the breezy charm and dry wit that were his in real life.

Another Powell and Pressburger film, Black Narcissus, featured David Farrar as 'strong, silent Mr Dean'. Tall, dark and handsome with a distinctive deep baritone voice, Farrar left England for Hollywood, but he never felt truly at home there and finally quit acting, saying: "I was afraid of parts being hinted at for uncles or the girl's father instead

The dark good looks of Dirk Bogarde made him a heartthrob

PICS: REX/SHUTTERSTOCK

Sean Connery made the role of 007 his own

Poetry Corner
Renewal and rebirth
By Amanda-Jayne Lanceley

I fling my windows wide open,
See winter has finally passed,
Gone is the snow and black ice,
The warmth of the sun here at last.

Bulbs laid dormant beneath me –
Push their green shoots through the earth,
Daffodils, snowdrops and tulips –
Once again erupt with new birth.

Apple trees clothed in blossom –
In colours of pale pink and white,
With bluebells, pansies and primrose,
Forming a wonderful sight.

Greenfinches sing in the treetops,
Back from migration once more,
Their song like harps softly strumming,
Drifts in through the open back door.

Days are now growing much longer,
As forward one hour the clocks go,
More time for enjoying the garden,
And giving the lawn its first mow.

The bumble bees are gathering –
Pollen from each little flower,
Pollinating each one they visit,
Working hard hour after hour.

Rebirth is here all around me,
In the fields lambs jump and play
Birds start gathering twigs and moss,
And soon their eggs they'll lay.

This is a season so special,
It really makes my heart sing,
When my garden bursts into life,
I know that it's finally spring.

of the lover."

Another Brit who was lured away by the American film industry was Stewart Granger who rose to fame as the romantic lead in a number of films for Gainsborough Pictures, the first of which was The Man in Grey. In 1949 he starred with Jean Simmons in the comedy Adam and Evelyne. She became his second wife before they both moved to Hollywood and appeared together again in the costume drama Young Bess. Christened James Leblanche Stewart, he took the name Granger to avoid confusion with James Stewart.

Born with an even more exotic name (Derek Jules Gaspard Ulric Niven van den Bogaerde), Dirk Bogarde got his break into films when Stewart Granger dropped out as the lead in Esther Waters. Following his debut, Bogarde signed a contract with J Arthur Rank, became a leading light in 'the Rank charm school' and the nation's heartthrob as Dr Simon Sparrow in the popular series of Doctor films. Who else could look as sexy wearing a sensible V-neck pullover with a shirt and tie?

But it was Richard Todd in Robin Hood and His Merrie Men who first alerted discerning fans to the joy of men in tights. Riding through the glen with his band of men, Todd cut a very fetching figure and it is no wonder that he was the first choice of author Ian Fleming for the role of James Bond. The course of film history might have been very different if Todd hadn't turned it down due to other commitments. But then we wouldn't have had one of the most popular poster boys ever, Sean Connery as 007!

PIC: ALAMY

Not all beer and skittle

Jackie Myers remembers five exhausting but amazing years as a pub landlady

Between 1977 and 1982 my 'vocation' in life was exhausting, stimulating, demanding and sometimes exasperating, but above all terribly amusing – running a pub in London's Islington district. Friends were amazed: "Going to run a pub – you're lucky, that's a real cushy job with lots of money to be made as well." Great I thought – when do I start.

It didn't turn out to be cushy at all, as I ended up being cook, waitress, barmaid, glass-washer, cleaner and general dogsbody. I had never worked so hard in my life! It also wasn't generally known, but a 'Mrs' working in a pub in those days, did not in fact get paid a salary, they called it an 'honorarium' which translates as 'not very much'.

Dealing with the public, though, did have many lighter moments. Misunderstandings happened if you were rushed and didn't listen properly. A customer of many years standing

ordered a pint of draught Guinness, with, I thought, 'a cherry'. In the belief that the customer is always right, I dutifully speared a cherry from the jar and plonked it in his pint. He nearly had apoplexy – the poor man had wanted 'a sherry'. It did look pretty against the white head of his Guinness though.

Tourists could be fun, usually appearing at the bar requesting, 'beer', not having fully understood our halves and pints system. I tended to demonstrate with my hands – saying: "Small one or big one?" Consequently they spent the rest of their trip entering pubs asking for 'beeg ones' and embarrassing other barmaids!

Being close to Sadler's Wells I also got a fair share of the theatre trade at night and while I had nothing against people with frilly shirts, bow ties and posh accents – they did try to impress fellow frilly shirts by being unnecessarily pompous. "Lager in a glass," was one order. I couldn't help wondering if he had previously been served his lager in a plastic bucket.

I also had customers who insisted on 'entertaining' other customers in the bar (whether they wanted it or not). Some would sing loudly (not necessarily the same tune that was playing on the jukebox) and some insisted on dancing around (when there was no music playing at all). There were those who used to stand on a chair and tell everyone their whole life story, and others who would swear at everybody and everything at the top of their voices.

One day I lost part of the building in an accident. A lady driver (sorry) careered into a parked car at speed, overturned her vehicle, and demolished the front porch and part of the corner wall of the public bar, finishing up slamming into a brick wall. Amazingly

Lovely day for a GUINNESS

Jackie discovered life behind the bar was not all about pouring the drinks – you had to be a good listener, too

she was unhurt but after much sweeping up of glass and picking up of debris, I asked the attending police officers how I could secure the pub for the night. Obviously much harassed, they replied that possibly a 'No Entry' sign on what was left of the entrance might be an idea – very helpful.

When the brewery or the government put the prices up in pubs, you would think it was my fault. Remarks such as, 'Saving up for a fur coat are we?' or, 'Going to the Bahamas for a holiday are we?' accompanied the moans and groans. Being a manager I had no control over the prices and had to charge as per instructions, so that made it worse.

Some customers, when ordering a round of drinks, would wave a vague hand around a packed bar and expect you to know who to include and who not to include, while others would hand you empty glasses and stammer: "Same again please" – when I hadn't served them before and didn't have a clue what they wanted.

Sometimes, it could be really quite boring. If you were behind the bar on your own, with very few customers to serve, there was nobody to talk to. When all the glasses were washed, all the ashtrays cleaned and tables wiped, there was nothing else to do. I would have brought the ironing board down from upstairs and finished the ironing if I thought I would get away with it.

It wasn't an easy thing, serving drinks, taking money, giving change etc, while being a social worker, medical advisor, psychoanalyst and marriage counsellor all rolled into one. Customers came in all shapes, sizes, colours and creeds and I tried to please some of them at least some of the time.

Next time you go out for the night, spare a thought for the 'Mrs' – it's not all beer and skittles. Having said that, I wouldn't have missed it for the world!

◆ Sadly, Jackie died in February 2015 – but her husband Evan said she would still have very much wished this story to be published.

A spring in her step

BY: CHRIS JAMES

A spring cleaning session has a romantic outcome

My daughter Ginny said: "If you haven't worn it in the last year it goes in the charity shop pile."

I replied: "That doesn't seem right. I've got clothes for hot weather – which we didn't have last summer – and various coats for other sorts of weather."

"Mum, I'm sure you've got coats that are older than I am!" laughed Ginny. "If Dad can sort out his stuff, so can you. Let's start with shoes. You need three piles; charity shop, keepers and 'thinking about'."

I opened my wardrobe with a heavy heart. There were boots that were too tight and shoes that were too loose. Any with broken heels or worn soles weren't good enough for the charity shop so that made four piles. Then there were my favourites, a bit shabby maybe, but comfortable.

Next we had to decide on the 'thinking about' pile. Ginny said: "Put them on and walk up and down, then I'll have the casting vote."

We giggled as I tottered about in a pair of stilettos. Ginny pointed firmly to the charity shop pile. These were followed by a pair of furry slippers that I'd been given for Christmas but never worn because I knew our dog would have loved to run off with them, given half a chance. Next we added a pair of red ballet pumps to the keepers.

So far, the decisions had been relatively easy. And as the floor of my wardrobe began to reappear I knew that Ginny was right. She exclaimed: "What are these?" as she pulled a box from the back of the cupboard. She lifted the lid and unwrapped the tissue paper. "Wow, these are stunning! Such soft leather. Where are they from?"

I sighed. "I hoped you might not find them. I bought them in a sale – the only luxury designer shoes I've ever owned. Since then I've been waiting for a special occasion to wear them, but it

'I hoped you might not find them. I bought them in a sale...'

never happened."

Optimistically, I slipped my feet into them but I knew at once I'd never be able to walk in them. I handed them to Ginny who peered inside to see the size. "They're way too small for me but too good for the charity shop," she said regretfully. "We'll put them in the 'thinking about' pile because you might sell them online. I'll put all of these in a bag in the spare room and we'll deal with it later."

At that moment my husband Dan came in from the garage. "Anyone want a coffee?" he asked, putting the kettle on.

After we'd all had a break, he said: "Have you got anything for recycling before I put the bins out? Then I'm off to town to drop my bags off at a charity shop."

Ginny grinned: "Put the bag of old shoes in with recycling before Mum changes her mind."

We went back upstairs to finish our task. While I returned the keepers to the wardrobe, she began sorting out the shoes for the charity shop and bagging them before we made a start on the clothes.

At long last, we were finished. "I think we deserve a glass of wine now," Ginny said as she led the way downstairs.

The next morning I had to smile when I opened my beautifully tidy wardrobe. While I was in this positive frame of mind, I decided to finish sorting through the 'thinking about' pile, but when I went into the spare room there was no bag to be seen.

I phoned Ginny. "I've looked everywhere," I told her. "Where did you put them?"

She said: "Didn't I put them in the spare room? Maybe I left them by the door?"

The thought dawned on both of us at the same time: "Dad!"

Dad defended himself: "Well, you said to put one bag out for recycling but, come to think of it, there was an extra bag when I dropped them off at the charity shop."

I called Ginny back at once and we both arrived at the charity shop at the same time. The lady behind the counter said: "A pair of designer shoes, size five? Yes, I remember them – they were so nice that we

sold them straightaway. A girl spotted them in the window and her boyfriend bought them for her."

Ginny put her arm through mine. "Sorry, Mum. Come on, I'll buy you a coffee and then we can go and look round the shoe shops for a pair of smart shoes that you can actually walk in."

We were halfway along the high street when Ginny suddenly stopped in her tracks and said: "Oh, would you look at that!"

An attractive young couple were walking towards us. She had her arm through his and was looking up at him adoringly. On her feet were my designer shoes.

"She looks as though she is walking on air," whispered Ginny. "She could be Cinderella with her prince!"

I chuckled delightedly. "Well, I guess that makes me a fairy godmother!"

We had stars in our eyes: LOVABLE ECCENTRICS

Kenneth Williams and Charles Hawtrey... dressed to arrest!

PICS REX SHUTTERSTOCK

They might not have had the star billing, but great character actors often stole the limelight. Who could possibly ignore burly, bearded James Robertson Justice striding down the wards of St Swithin's hospital followed by a gaggle of nervous medical students? The role of Sir Lancelot Spratt perfectly suited an actor who was equally ebullient off-screen – he fought in the Spanish Civil War, stood for Parliament under an assumed Gaelic name and was said to count Prince Philip among his friends.

Terry Thomas played the bounder to perfection

In complete contrast, Charles Hawtrey played weedy individuals who blinked worriedly at life through round National Health spectacles. A stalwart of the Carry On films, Hawtrey earned the title King of Camp for scenes like the one in Carry On Constable in which he and Kenneth Williams are undercover policemen who dress up as women (calling themselves Ethel and Agatha) in a failed, but very funny, attempt to catch suspected shoplifters.

If Hawtrey was far from being a ladies' man, gap-toothed Terry Thomas was the epitome of the smooth-talking seducer. He perfected his persona of a moustache-twirling cad in Carlton-Browne of the FO and went on to reprise it in many more films including School for Scoundrels in which he wins a blatantly unfair tennis match against his rival in love, Ian Carmichael. 'Jolly good show' and 'You're an absolute shower' were among Terry Thomas's familiar catchphrases. A flashy dresser on and off screen, he invariably sported a carnation in his buttonhole and wore fancy waistcoats (of which he owned 150!)

Also fond of sporting a natty waistcoat, worn with a bow tie, was larger-than-life actor Robert Morley. Of portly build with double chins and bushy eyebrows, Morley was no matinée idol but was perfectly cast as a jovial, pompous chap with a plummy accent in

Margaret Rutherford was at home playing slightly dotty ladies

Poetry Corner

The postman needs to call twice!

By Beryl Earnshaw

Say 'hullo' to your postman, he'll be bringing you stacks
Of leaflets on stair-lifts and funeral packs.
Life-time insurance, 'No medical required',
Oh yes, we are popular once we've retired.

Info on wheelchairs and equity release
Vitamins and diet foods for thin and obese.
Denture enhancement, supports for the knees
Things to make sure you don't leak when you sneeze.

Top cures for baldness and hair-dyes for men
Promise to make us look 40 again.
Shavers for ladies to rid us of 'taches,
And creams to prevent any after-shave rashes

In-your-face prompters, 'Have you made your will?'
Might just as well tell us, 'You're over the hill'.
Well, we've all had enough, on your bikes,
you're not funny,
Now, let me get back to my All-Bran and honey.

But ah, 'Fabulous cruises to exotic locations'
Convince us we need to make reservations.
For wall-to-wall sun where we won't need a brolly,
Alas, what we will need – a shed full of lolly!

So just for the moment, let's think of the plusses
Avoiding the rush-hour, free travel on buses.
We'll travel this island from Cape Wrath to Dover,
A gap year we'll call it – become a wild rover.

We can't turn the clock back, but hey, does it matter?
We're all getting older, forgetful and fatter.
So what if our wrinkles are longer and deeper?
At least we can go places a helluva lot cheaper!

PIC: SHUTTERSTOCK

films such as Ladies Who Do and Curtain Up. In a TV interview with Simon Dee he cheerfully admitted to being a lifelong gambler, frequently betting on the horses with his friend and fellow punter, Wilfrid Hyde-White.

Hyde-White usually played gentle, well-intentioned souls such as kindly Colonel Pickering in My Fair Lady. Like many of the screen's lovable eccentrics, he mostly played versions of himself. He claimed: "I learned two things at drama school: first, that I couldn't act; second, that it didn't matter."

Not all our lovable eccentrics were men – dear old ladies often steal the show in British films. Katie Johnson will always be remembered as Mrs Wilberforce, the genteel widow in The Ladykillers, who innocently harbours a gang of crooks in her run-down London boarding house. Blissfully unaware, Mrs Wilberforce escapes her lodgers' increasingly desperate attempts to do away with her and eventually she inherits their ill-gotten gains.

Margaret Rutherford carved out a splendid career playing dotty ladies of a certain age. She imbued Madame Arcati, the medium in Noel Coward's Blithe Spirit, with her own glorious brand of eccentricity. Clad in no-nonsense tweeds and a cape, she is seen cycling serenely along country lanes when she is not conducting séances to be rid of that mischievous ghost, Elvira. Rutherford also put her unique stamp on Agatha Christie's Miss Marple, sleuth and spinster of the parish of St Mary Mead. In real life, Rutherford was not a spinster but happily married to actor Stringer Davis who appeared in many of her films.

Sand and batter never

Nothing could top a summer trip to the seaside with the local working men's club, remembers Allan T Konury

The Beatles, Adam Faith and crazy fashions are just some of the fond memories I have of the Sixties. As a young boy, along with my little brother and our parents, the annual club trip to the coast was surely one of the highlights of the year.

At about eight o'clock on a Sunday morning, the convoy of coaches outside the local working men's club would soon be full of excited families, all ready for the journey to either Mablethorpe or Skegness – the most popular of all the destinations. It would only take about one-and-a-half hours from our little village in South Yorkshire.

Organised by the committee, the coaches had already been loaded with crates of pop and boxes of crisps for the trip. Just before we set off, the club secretary would come on each of the coaches and hand all the children an envelope containing ten shillings – your pocket money for the day. This came out of the club funds Dad would have paid into weekly.

We always sat in a row in front of Mum and Dad, but you would always get some of the teenagers making a beeline for the back seats. During the journey they would be waving to any passing motorist hoping to get a wave and

a smile back. The journey soon passed and as the convoy neared the coast we could smell the sea, the fish and chips, doughnuts and candy floss.

We came from a very close mining community, so it wasn't unusual for everyone to stay together. We found a space on the beach to set up camp and while my brother and I, along with some of the other kids, went off to explore the crab pools, some of the dads would go to fetch the deckchairs. There must have been a dozen or so and these would be put in a large circle for the parents to sit on. We children

mix

Allan (above right) was three years older than his brother but they both looked forward to their seaside day trips

didn't need any, for there was far too much for us to do.

The warm summer sun would beat down on us, so Mum would make sure we had plenty of sun cream on. Horrible, sticky stuff. Most of the day was spent on the beach, collecting crabs and shells, building sandcastles and making little ditches for the sea to run into when the tide came in. The football match between the mums and dads with the young ones just joining in, was sure to be a highlight of the day. We went with the winning side, which was usually the mums. (I'm sure they were allowed to win!)

After all the fun and running about, we sure worked up a good appetite, so it was Mum's job to go to the fish shop, which was only a little way from the beach. We looked forward to our dinner because there is nothing quite like

fresh fish and chips in the open air, but were careful not to drop our fish. Sand and better never go well together. After dinner, a little relaxing time was needed. Our parents would just chat with each other while we went of exploring some more pools and had a paddle in the sea.

For the last hour or two, before the journey home, we would take a gentle stroll around the shops for little souvenirs and, of course, sticks of rock and bars of nougat. Mum did a little bit of shopping while Dad always ended up carrying the bags. This was his main role in life, he would say.

We would be tired but happy by the end of the day. The sun always seemed to shine in summer in those days – that's how I remember it anyway.

By five o'clock it would be time

to head back to the coach for the journey home with everyone chatting about the day we'd just had. The coach driver would put the radio on and it was usually something like, Sing Something Simple. It wasn't long before the younger ones would be asleep – it was generally quieter going home than the trip there.

Back at the club, some of the trippers would get all their belongings from the coach, saying, 'Goodbye, see you later', (which was often that night in the club). Some people would be nursing sunburn, others aching legs from all the walking. But there was never any trouble – everyone would always be on their best behaviour.

Oh happy memories. And straightaway we would start looking forward to the next trip – wherever that was going to be.

Close of play

BY: KAY SEELEY

Rosemary finds a way to keep up Aunt Bessie's tradition

Rosemary's heart pounded. She couldn't believe what she was hearing. "What do you mean, retire?" she demanded. "I bin doing cricket teas in Oakington since I was old enough to lift a kettle." Anger swelled inside her. "There's nowt wrong with my teas. Famous they are. Famous."

Ted twisted his cap awkwardly in his hands. "I'm sorry, Rosemary, it's the committee, see…"

"The committee be blowed!" she glared at the hapless Ted. "It's them incomers. Taking over the village, they are. Well, we'll see about that."

Eyes blazing, she stripped off her apron and pushed Ted out of the door. Twenty minutes later she was making tea for Bill Hathaway, former captain of Oakington cricket team.

"I bin helping with cricket teas for nigh on fifty years," she said to the kindly old man. "Aunt Bessie did them then. She weren't never asked to retire. They wouldn't have dared."

Bill nodded. "She were a formidable woman, your Aunt Bessie. She wouldn't let nowt disrupt her teas. Not the war, not rationing. Without fail, she'd produce a spread that was the envy of the county. Them were the days."

Rosemary handed him a plate of biscuits. "And what do I get? Retire! Retire when I'm in me prime."

"Nowt I can do, lass, not since that Nick took over the captaincy. I was pushed out for the price of an electric scoreboard and new sightscreens." Bill shook his head. "Of course, it's his missus that wants to run things. She had a falling out with old George at the pub. Said he should be serving macrobiotic food! George gave her a right flea in her ear! Now she wants to take over the cricket teas."

On her way home, Rosemary brooded over the coming season. She loved the unchanging ritual of

When the village team was winning, Rosemary was in seventh heaven

cricket; the smell of freshly mown grass, the crack of leather on willow, the players' appreciation of her famous teas. Her family might laugh at her, but on a warm summer evening when the village team was winning, Rosemary was in her seventh heaven.

Her thoughts turned to the newcomers. Nick and his wife Fiona had bought the manor house after the death of the old colonel. They made no attempt to hide their belief that a fat wallet compensated for centuries of tradition. One of their first moves had been to reroute the right of way that ran through their woods so that walkers were forced to make a lengthy detour along the main road. Then their helipad made them unpopular with many of their neighbours.

When the colonel was alive, Rosemary had worked at the manor house and she still had a cleaning job there a couple of mornings a week. She had observed the many changes Fiona had made, announcing loudly that she wanted to live in a modern home, not a museum.

When they had dinner parties, Rosemary was asked to help out in the kitchen, but not to serve at the table. Fiona felt this would lower the tone. Fiona was very keen on tone, Rosemary noticed. However, not wishing to risk losing her part-time job, she swallowed her pride and offered to give Fiona a hand with preparing the tea for the opening match of the season.

"No, thank you," Fiona said. "It's all sorted and packed away in the freezer. But I do need you to do kitchen duty for the eve-of-match dinner party I'm giving for some of Nick's business associates. I've prepared a macrobiotic menu: fried soba sushi in broth, aduki bean rice and roast pepper couscous."

Rosemary shuddered at the thought, but the evening went better than she would have predicted. Fiona's 'balanced symphony of seasonal fare' appeared to go down well with the slick city types. From the kitchen she could hear the hum of conversation punctuated by bursts of laughter and the clink of glasses.

ILLUSTRATION: KATE DAVIES

Before going home she boiled the kettle and prepared the dandelion tea

Before going home to her cottage she boiled the kettle and prepared the dandelion tea which Fiona claimed was 'more refreshing and better for you than caffeinated tea'.

The next morning dawned bright with the promise of a fine day of sunshine. Rosemary smiled as she looked out of her bedroom window. Perfect weather for the opening match of the season, she thought with satisfaction.

The telephone rang and she hurried downstairs to answer it. It was Ted. He said: "It's an emergency! Can you do the cricket tea at short notice? Fiona, Nick and half their guests have gone down with a stomach bug. You're our only hope, Rosemary, forget all that talk about retiring."

Rosemary said: "Oh dear, poor Fiona. Ain't that a shame. Of course I won't let you down."

She glanced into the dining room at the table laden with sausage rolls, pork pies, fancy cakes and scones with cream and jam. That just left the sandwiches to make, nice and fresh. Her heart swelled with happiness at the thought of another year of making the cricket teas.

Smiling to herself, she thought, 'I knew Aunt Bessie's laxative powders would come in handy one day'.

We had stars in our eyes:
COMIC CROOKS

Ronald Shiner, Sid James and Brian Rix in the film Dry Rot

The criminal classes loom large in many of the films that we look back on as a golden age of British comedy. Long before he was shady Arthur Daley in the TV series Minder, George Cole brought laughter to our lives as the lovable rogue, Flash Harry, in the St Trinian's films. Emerging from the shrubbery with his collar turned up, hands thrust deep in his pockets, Harry is always on hand to assist the schoolgirls in their nefarious activities… selling the gin they distil in the chemistry lab, placing their bets on the horses, as well as running a marriage bureau to find wealthy husbands for the sixth formers.

Harry's matchmaking skills might well have been welcomed by fellow St Trinian's star Joyce Grenfell who, as gawky WP Sergeant Ruby Gates, yearns for her reluctant fiancé Superintendent Kemp-Bird to name the day. The local constabulary are no match for the school's pupils and their equally immoral teachers. All too often Ruby's toothy smile wavers and fades in disbelief as they – and the men from the Ministry of Education – are outwitted once again.

Another great comic actor, Peter Sellers, found early fame as a crook before he became even more famous as the inept detective Clouseau. Sellers was violin-playing Harry in the gang of thieves in The Ladykillers, while in Two Way Stretch he plays the supposedly model prisoner Dodger Lane who plans the perfect robbery with two fellow insiders, the aptly named Jelly Knight (David Lodge) and Lennie Price (Bernard Cribbins) before the arrival of a strict new head guard Sidney 'Sour' Crout (Lionel Jefferies) throws their scheme into disarray.

Another Flash Harry pops up in Dry Rot in which three dishonest bookies try to rig a race by kidnapping the favourite horse and its jockey. Sid James (who surely had the wickedest chortle in showbusiness) is Harry and his partners in crime are Fred Phipps (Brian Rix) and Alf Tubbe (Ronald Shiner).

George Cole was the perfect Flash Harry

Peter Sellers and
Bernard Cribbins team
up in Two Way Stretch

Poetry Corner

Too much, too late

By Carol Turner

A man that you love, kids on the way
Money so tight that there's no time to play
Mortgage so high that you eat beans on toast
And gaze at the butcher, whilst craving a roast.
School trips and uniforms, holidays too
At times not enough for a trip round the zoo.
Easter and Christmas, never a break
Must find the right toys or their hearts will so ache.
Uni, plus fees, and then comes that gap year
They travel the world never knowing the fear
That grabs at your heart as you wave them goodbye
They have to move on, give their lives a good try.
Marriage is next; my that costs you a bomb
And that's when it hits you, the kids are all gone.

Stop...

This is the part that's confusing as hell
Money's abundant, you're doing quite well
The mortgage is paid; you can buy a new house
Not be stuck in a place where you can't swing a mouse.
Best steak for dinner, eat out once a week
You shop now in style, it's not bargains you seek.
Retirement is great as you travel the world
And gaze round in wonder as sights are unfurled
It's then you come home, to the new empty house
Where you don't want to be, nor be swinging a mouse
Why wasn't it there when the kids were all small?
Where was all this then, when you needed it all?
With time to reflect, you could wish you'd done more
But it wasn't to be, and the kids know the score
But there's joy to be found, even on this late day
For the grandkids can come
and there's more room for play.

Not the brightest fraudsters on the block, their daft idea to conceal the horse in the cellar of their hotel could have been pinched from The Belles of St Trinian's in which the fourth-formers hide kidnapped racehorse Arab Boy in their dormitory. But the bookies' ambitious plan is doomed when their case is taken on by Sergeant Fire, played by everybody's favourite battleaxe, Peggy Mount.

Another actress who frequently played battleaxes, Hattie Jacques, turned to crime for a charitable cause in Make Mine Mink. As Nanette Parry, she embarks on a spree of stealing fur coats along with fellow boarding-house residents Dame Beatrice Appleby (Athene Seyler) and Elizabeth Pinkie Pinkerton (Elspeth Duxbury). Under the guidance of Major Albert Payne (Terry-Thomas), they are very successful until they are 'sussed' by their devoted maid and reformed con (Billie Whitelaw) who – inconveniently for the gang – falls in love with a policeman.

No round-up of comic criminals would be complete without mention of The Lavender Hill Mob, a jewel in the crown of Ealing comedies. Alfie Bass and Sid James are the professional thieves who assist bank employee Henry Holland (Alec Guinness) and his accomplice Alfred Pendlebury (Stanley Holloway) in their plan to smuggle gold bullion out of the country disguised as replicas of the Eiffel Tower. They are such a likeable bunch and their plan so ingenious that you can't help hoping that they will get away with it.

PIC: SHUTTERSTOCK

Happy days in

Some of the many visitors in the garden of the boarding house. Below Ruth having left school and inset present day

Ruth Spencer remembers a magical wartime childhood even though she was living in 'Hellfire Corner'

"You'll be sleeping in the attic bedroom tonight. I've put your things in there," my mother said when I got home from school. The information didn't trouble me. The attic bedroom had windows on two sides: one looking out over the English Channel and the other across the Romney Marshes. I loved the room but my sleeping quarters weren't always at the top of the house. They could have been anywhere in our seaside home in the village of Dymchurch.

Shortly before the outbreak of the Second World War my mother achieved her dream of buying somewhere to run a boarding house. She couldn't have chosen a time more unsuitable for such a venture. Our part of Kent became known as Hellfire Corner. Dymchurch was well-known for its stretches of safe, golden sand, and earned the title of Children's

Paradise. During the summer months, the village welcomed all kinds of holiday-makers. They stayed in caravans and on campsites, hotels and bed and breakfast accommodation, as well as boarding houses.

That was before 1939. When the dark clouds of war gathered there was no way down to the sand. The famous sea wall was festooned with barbed wire and armed soldiers stood on guard. My mother had to accept the fact that she would not be caring for families with buckets and spades and swimwear. She had to accept something else – the arrival of men who were to work on the drainage of the Marsh.

As well as three or four workmen, others were billeted with us, among them a local schoolteacher. The house was always overflowing with people

and this meant there were often rearrangements to be made about who slept where. Hence my constant change of bedrooms.

The Battle of Britain was fought above our heads, and all around was evidence of warfare on the land.

bad times

Ruth age 12

Soldiers camped in fields and their lorries were constantly trundling along the road as an accompaniment to everyday life. Fred Brown was the only one of our lodgers who was in the Home Guard. He had a rifle, although I am not sure if he knew how to use it. It stood in our hall and Fred told my mother that she was to pick it up and threaten any enemy soldier who might appear. It was all very much like Dad's Army and we gave the rifle a wide berth when going through the hall.

Dymchurch School was not open every day of the week. The education of the village children, from infants up to the leaving age of 14, was put in the hands of Edith Weth, a formidable little lady of less than five feet tall, whose methods were anything but orthodox. Her task was not an easy one; bringing some order to the lives of the many youngsters whose parents had chosen not to have them evacuated. But she did it with a style which inspired us in a way which far more traditionally accepted teachers could ever have done.

With practically no equipment with which to work, she talked us through history, geography and English literature. This suited the girls as, while we listened, we knitted endless scarves, socks and Balaclava helmets in thick blue wool – clothing for the Navy.

Bombs fell on the village. One of my school friends, Peggy Breeze, lived with her grandmother and a great aunt in Dymchurch High Street and, when their cottage was bombed, they all came to join our household. Aunty was very old indeed, crippled and almost blind. Although we did our best to make her feel at home, to begin with she hated being with us. One of her many attempts to escape could have been a part of a Carry On film. Our milkman carried his churns in the sidecar of a motorcycle. On a morning delivery, Aunty crawled out to him and pleaded with him to take her home on the back seat of his motorcycle. After several weeks, the three of them were able to return to their cottage and by that time Aunty had become very happy where she was. So much so, that she cried when she had to leave us.

Supper was a time of day which I recall with pleasure. We were such a mixed collection of people, brought together by war. When the supper things were cleared away, we played cards until it was time to hear the news on the wireless or listen to ITMA, Tommy Handley's popular radio show at the time. I was the only child in the household and I was probably the only child in the area who played cards for money with men and sometimes won. Big stakes were involved – as much as 2d and 3d!

After the war my mother did get visitors with bathing costumes and buckets and spades – but somehow it was never quite the same.

A grand day out

BY: PAMELA HIBBERT

Rose hopes Arthur won't spoil her day at the seaside

The coach pulled out of the drive of The Cosy Nook care home, its passengers full of eager anticipation. Joanna, an enthusiastic young carer, trilled into the microphone: "We're all going to have a really brill day in Scarborough!"

There were murmurs of agreement as she took her seat.

"Silly cow," Arthur muttered to Rose, sitting next to him. "Talks like we're a bunch of seven year olds. And what's 'brill' when it's at home? Sounds like something you clean pans with."

He removed his glasses and polished them with a spotless white handkerchief.

"Relax, Arthur," said Rose.

"I've not come to relax. I've come out to have a damn good time."

"If that means what I think it means, you'll be sat on your own on the way back," Rose warned. Arthur enjoyed a pint or three when he could escape Joanna's gimlet gaze.

"I'm not going to bingo and I'm not going to sit on the beach all day watching yon madam trying to organise daft games," he grumbled.

Rose sighed. She wondered why she had agreed to come on an outing with Arthur. Again. Still, even Arthur's moaning was livelier than being stuck in The Cosy Nook all day watching the telly.

"Have you got any of them mints?" Arthur interrupted her thoughts. She found a packet in her bag and offered him one. They sucked the sweets in companionable silence.

Rose looked out of the window. She still found it exciting to catch the first glimpse of the sea. It reminded her of day trips to Filey when she was a child. Since those days Rose had been abroad on holiday but she still thought you couldn't beat the English seaside on a sunny day. She hoped Arthur

She still thought you couldn't beat the English seaside on a sunny day

was going to cheer up, bless him.

"You know what, Rose, I reckon you and me could do worse than, you know, get together." Arthur patted her on the knee.

Rose spluttered as her mint went down the wrong way. "You can stop that business," she said. "I'm going on the pier."

"Just what I had in mind," said Arthur.

When the coach stopped, Joanna stood up. "Back here at seven, everyone, and don't leave anything on the coach. Have a nice day!"

"American nonsense!" muttered Arthur.

"If you're going to have that attitude, I'm off," Rose said, but they strolled together to the pier. The sun felt warm on their faces and Arthur bought two ice-cream cornets. They leaned on the railing and watched a large container ship moving slowly across the horizon.

"I wanted to go to sea," said Arthur. "But I had to join the family business. Greengrocer was me dad."

"I never knew that."

Arthur grunted. Rose studied his face. For a moment, he seemed as far away as the ship and she sensed his regret. She said: "When you get to our age there's all that looking back on what we might have been or done. It's pointless. My son says we should regret the things we've done, not the ones we didn't do."

"Well, I've plenty of them!" Arthur said. "Things I've done, I mean."

Rose wondered what they might be and thought there was more to Arthur than his grumpiness.

After fish and chips for lunch, they played a round of mini-golf. Rose won easily. "Right, the tea and cakes are on you," Arthur said.

As they sat in the café, glad to take the weight off their feet, Rose decided to seize the moment. She asked: "So what are these things you regret doing?"

"Now there's a question. I'm not sure as you'd really want to know."

"Try me." Rose topped up their tea from the pot.

"The thing I most regret is…" Arthur hesitated. "You're not going to approve of this."

ILLUSTRATION: KATE DAVIES

'Folk didn't get divorced then, not like they do now. They put up with things'

Rose reached across the table and touched his hand.

"What I most regret is marrying who I did. I mean, she was a real looker was Meg, but once the ring was on her finger she turned into a right shrew. Always on about summat. Always on at me and the two boys, never any peace."

Rose didn't know what to say, so she said nothing.

"Folk didn't get divorced then, not like they do now. They put up with things."

"Yes, they did," said Rose, who had memories and some regrets of her own.

They finished their tea and polished off the scones.

"Come on then," said Arthur. "Let's go and have a paddle."

For once, he didn't want to go to the pub. Instead, they sat on a seafront bench and watched the tide coming in and the fairy lights twinkling on the South Bay.

"It's been a grand day," said Arthur.

"Yes, it has," agreed Rose.

On the coach they made their way to the back seat. "Where the naughty kids always sat!" laughed Rose.

Someone started up a sing-song. Arthur turned to Rose and she was smiling at him. He took her hand and tucked it under his arm. And there it remained, all the way back to The Cosy Nook.

We had stars in our eyes:
GLAMOUR GIRLS

Jean Simmons headed off to Hollywood

Diana Dors was the British answer to Marilyn Monroe

Joan Greenwood's love scene with Dennis Price was considered steamy

PICS: REX SHUTTERSTOCK

Sultry brunettes, ravishing redheads and blonde bombshells – British films boasted a bevy of beautiful leading ladies. Not surprisingly, Hollywood beckoned to many of them, most memorably Vivien Leigh who shot to stardom when she was cast as Scarlett in Gone with the Wind, despite keen competition from more established American actresses.

Similarly, after appearing in films such as the thriller So Long at the Fair and Powell and Pressburger's Black Narcissus Jean Simmons left the UK with husband Stewart Granger and soon achieved international fame as demure Sergeant Sarah Brown in the Hollywood musical Guys and Dolls.

Not to be outdone by curvy American pin-up girls, we had our own home-grown versions. Busty platinum blonde Diana Dors (born in Swindon) claimed to be the English answer to Marilyn Monroe, while the equally voluptuous Sabrina (born in Stockport) was said to be a shoo-in for

Jayne Mansfield.

Diana's private life was even more racy then her screen image and she was sternly denounced as 'a wayward hussy' by the Archbishop of Canterbury. Sabrina, perhaps wisely, chose to be a dumb blonde who opted for non-speaking parts like the one in Blue Murder at St Trinian's in which she was simply required to look desirable in a nightdress.

But how many actresses could look as desirable in a sweaty khaki uniform as Sylvia Syms did struggling across the desert in Ice Cold in Alex? With her sleeves rolled up to her elbows and her shirt tied casually at the waist, she found herself attracted to the flawed officer, played by John Mills.

Shirley Eaton started her career as a pretty starlet who graced many British films in the 1950s and 1960s including many of the box-office hits in the Doctor in the House and Carry On comedies. Her moment of enduring fame came in 1964 when she was 007's unfortunate girlfriend painted from head to toe in gold paint in Goldfinger. However,

Kay Kendall with Kenneth More in the film Genevieve

Poetry Corner

First Great Grandchild (not yet born)

By P W Wheeler

May you be a beautiful or handsome baby
When you arrive, all soft and new
Great Nan and I will love you
Be you pink or be you blue

May you always love Mum, Holly,
May you always love Dad ,Steve,
May you always walk an honest path
And wear your heart upon your sleeve

May you always do for others
What others do for you
May you have a good sense of humour
Be you pink or be you blue

May you always be courageous
May you always be bold
Keep your family tight around you
For they are all touched with gold

May you always help others
Who are not as lucky as you
May your mind always be open
Be you pink or be you blue

May your life be full of laughter
May your health always be sound
May your judgement always be valid
By keeping your feet upon the ground

May your heart always be open
For those who share your view
May you always be successful
Be you pink or be you blue

May your hands always be nimble
May your feet always be swift
Raise your children lovingly
Because they are a special gift

Life will not always be acceptable
But I will tell you something that's true
Great Nan and I will always love you
Be you pink or be you blue.

PIC: SHUTTERESTOCKK

Shirley preferred the role of mum to being a Bond girl, saying: "A career is a career, but you're a mother until you die."

Both Glynis Johns and Joan Greenwood will always be remembered for their deliciously husky voices. Greenwood appeared in several of the best-known Ealing comedies including Whisky Galore! and The Man in the White Suit. Her (fully clothed) love scene with Dennis Price was almost cut from Kind Hearts and Coronets as it was considered too steamy by Michael Balcon, the head of Ealing Studios. How times have changed!

Long before she played the children's mother in Mary Poppins, Glynis Johns charmed filmgoers in the unlikely role of a flirtatious mermaid in Miranda and the follow-up Mad About Men. Her distinctive voice inspired Stephen Sondheim to write Send on the Clowns which she performed in A Little Night Music on Broadway.

Combining slender good looks with a gift for comedy, Kay Kendall brought a vivacious sense of humour to many films. She won a Golden Globe for her performance as Lady Sybil in the musical Les Girls but maybe her finest moment was in Genevieve in which she plays Kenneth More's elegant girlfriend Rosalind. En route to Brighton in the annual veteran car race, they stop at a hotel where Rosalind has a few too many and, to the amazement of her companions, insists in playing the trumpet with the hotel's jazz band before falling into an inebriated sleep.

A child of Variety

Josephine Bretherton grew up steeped in the magic of Music Hall artistes

Josephine's Uncle Tom Moss, left, and right, her dad, Joe

"A funny thing happened on my way to the theatre tonight, my wife gave birth to a bouncing baby girl." These were my father's opening lines to the theatre audience on the night of my birth. As a little girl I would listen enthralled whenever Dad recounted the story. It was 1940, due to heavy enemy bombardment; my birth took place in the cellar of my grandma's home in the midlands. The doctor who attended Mum was unable to leave for home during the bombing raid as it was unsafe to be outdoors. So the story goes that Grandma and the doctor toasted my birth by drinking whisky until the all clear was sounded.

In the Forties, most towns had a theatre. My father and his elder brother were Music Hall artistes and comedians, so they travelled from town to town entertaining audiences. Families travelled the length and breadth of the country along with them, obviously living out of suitcases, which must have been exhausting for wives and mothers, a fact that only occurred to me when I became a mum.

After the war there were weekly shows, revues, performances on seaside piers, all glamorous events for a young child. I never once got bored watching or listening to the shows that my father appeared in. I knew his jokes off by heart, but still found them highly amusing and laughed at each one. I was particularly fond of watching the chorus girls dancing and often peeked into their dressing rooms backstage. The chorus girls were very kind allowing me to join in their dance rehearsals. I can remember the smell of the grease paint, the tangible feeling of excitement as performers waited for their turn to perform on stage.

My all-time favourite was pantomime. Dad played the dame and his brother played Buttons. Auntie Valerie was always the good fairy. Under

Josephine, left and above, with one of Cinderella's ponies

school age, I was allowed to watch every single matinée. Being dropped off at the front door of the theatre I would find my way to my reserved front row seat. I remember one scene where Dad, playing the dame, lost one of his legs, obviously a false one. I was horrified and cried all the way back to Dad's dressing room. He showed me that his own leg was still intact to avoid further tears.

My dad loved telling me stories of showbusiness and related his experience when they went on the wireless during the war. Prior to the broadcast, everyone had to hand in their scripts to the censor whose job it was to check everything before it went live over the airwaves.

Performers knew it was vital that scripts had to be adhered to meticulously Anyone who forgot their lines, changed words in any shape or form or even paused, would immediately be blacked out in case that person was sending coded messages to the enemy.

One evening, as a special treat we were taken to an evening performance. Seated in a grand box overlooking the stage we watched as a couple began to dance to dramatic music; they wore Parisian outfits. The dance had the man flinging his partner across the stage with pretend contempt. The lady would re-approach him meekly only to have him repeat the performance of throwing her around the stage in time to the music. My three-year-old sister took offence at these proceedings. Standing at the front of the box she yelled at the man on the stage for all she was worth for him to 'leave that lady alone and get off her'. As our box was situated next to a microphone everyone heard my sister's words. She literally brought the house down, the show ground to a halt as the audience gave way to uproarious laughter. The manager asked to borrow my sister for the next performance to repeat her outburst.

After the war, live entertainment declined as the film industry took over and theatres were forced to close. Our local Hippodrome became a supermarket. At five years of age I started school, which curtailed my previous freedom. Famous people still visited, arriving by car or taxi, a fact I took for granted. It never occurred to me that others did not have access to travel by car. To my mind it was only natural to call a taxi to get home. I recall my friend and I, both nine years of age, attending a school gala evening. As we left the building to return home I naturally approached the taxi rank with my friend in tow who was scandalised at what she thought was cheek on my part. I spoke to a taxi driver, offering him sixpence to take us home by taxi and he did. Happy memories indeed.

PIC: REX SHUTTERSTOCK

Going it alone

BY: PENNY PECORELLI

Sam has trouble understanding his feisty grandma

Sam backed away from the man and the woman who were glaring at him in disgust. "You should be ashamed of yourself, young man!"

"But, but…" he stammered.

"Letting that old lady carry that suitcase all by herself. What are you thinking?"

Sam blushed to the roots of his hair, but said nothing. It was hopeless to try to explain to strangers how stubborn his grandmother was. Every time anyone tried to help her, even if it was to take her arm when walking down steps, she would snap: "I can manage perfectly well, thank you. What do you think I am? Old?"

The couple went on their way and Sam hurried after the small woman who was slowly dragging her suitcase along the platform. By the time he caught up with her she had stopped to rest.

He tried once again. "Are you sure I can't put that on the train for you?"

"I'm fine," she said firmly, "just catching my breath."

He saw her settled in her window seat and waved goodbye as the train pulled out of the station. When he arrived home, Sam slumped down at the kitchen table.

His mother asked: "What's up with you? Did you see Grandma off all right?"

Sam told her what had happened.

"Oh dear, poor you," his mother said wryly. "Mum has always been strong-willed. Dad used to just let her have her own way – it was useless to argue – but I have to say I've noticed she has got worse recently. I think she's frightened of losing her independence and being a burden."

Sam said: "I suppose so, but it was embarrassing. All those people could see was a strapping young man letting a frail old lady struggle with a suitcase.

'I think she is frightened of losing her independence and being a burden'

I can see their point!"

His mother went on: "In some ways being stubborn is a good thing. It keeps her going. And she's not one to sit around like some older folk."

A week away with her sister did his grandmother good. When she returned to her granny annexe she was feistier than ever.

Then an unexpected disaster struck. It wasn't his grandmother who suffered a fall, but Sam. He was playing football when a particularly vicious tackle knocked him to the ground where he lay in agonising pain. He was vaguely aware of the other players standing around him looking concerned before the ambulance came and took him to the hospital.

When he came round from the anaesthetic, he found himself in bed with his leg up in traction. Sam had never felt so helpless in his life.

He was horrified when a middle-aged nurse approached him, saying briskly: "Come on, luvvie. Let's give you a wash."

A wash! Even his own mother hadn't given him a wash since he'd started school. He shut his eyes and endured the humiliation as best he could.

"We've just got to make you nice and fresh. Don't worry, luvvie. I've seen it all before."

Gritting his teeth, Sam muttered: "That's as may be, but it's not something I'm used to…"

Overcome with frustration, he wondered how long it would be before he was able to do things for himself again. As if reading his thoughts, the nurse dried his toes with a towel and said: "In a couple of months you'll be as right as rain."

A couple of months! How on earth would he survive that long, unable even to pour himself a glass of water? In the following weeks, he found he was totally reliant on the staff and his visitors for almost everything.

It gave Sam plenty of time to think. For the first time he had an insight into how his grandmother must feel when people fussed around her, making her an object of pity instead of the strong,

ILLUSTRATION: KATE DAVIES

Having to rely on other people was demoralising – frightening even

independent person she had always been. Now he understood what his mother had meant when she'd tried to explain Grandma's feelings. Having to rely on other people was demoralising – frightening even.

At last he was allowed home. Before he left, the staff taught him how to use his crutches and warned him against putting any weight on the injured leg. He was given a follow-up appointment. "After that, physio!" the doctor said cheerfully.

It felt wonderful to be back in the kitchen, sitting at the table drinking coffee with his grandmother. She said: "Oh dear, it must have been terrible for you. Does it still hurt?"

He admitted that it did. "But they've given me some painkillers. I go back in a month and then I'll have physio. It means I'll miss all the summer sports," he said glumly.

"Ah, but look on the bright side," his grandmother said, "you'll have plenty of time to study for your exams."

"Thanks, Grandma, that's really cheered me up!" Sam stood carefully and reached for his crutches.

"Let me help you!" his grandmother cried.

"No, it's all right. I can manage," he insisted.

"You'll fall!"

"I said I can manage. I have to learn."

"You're so stubborn," she said. "Won't accept help from anyone. I don't know where you get it from."

We had stars in our eyes:
THE BADDIES

Robert Newton as the unpleasant Bill Sikes in Oliver Twist

PICS: REX SHUTTERSTOCK

Arch-villain Herbert Lom once commented: "In English eyes, all foreigners are sinister." Born in Czechoslovakia, he never lost his foreign accent which served him in good stead in his many menacing roles that included being the scariest member of the gang in The Ladykillers, as well as the title part in the Hammer horror The Phantom of the Opera. Although he made a convincing baddie, Lom is affectionately remembered for his hilarious portrayal of Inspector Clouseau's boss, Commissioner Charles Dreyfus.

In the Hammer horror film, Count Dracula, Lom played opposite Christopher Lee, another fine actor who made his name playing villainous characters. In a long career, he played the blood-sucking vampire Count Dracula ten times and the evil Dr Fu Manchu five times. At 6ft 5in, he towered over most of his co-stars including Peter Cushing with whom he appeared in a total of 24 films. Off screen the two men were lifelong friends.

Famous as Frankenstein, Cushing once said: "I have either been a monster-maker or a monster-destroyer, but never a monster. Actually, I'm a gentle fellow. Never harmed a fly."

That certainly couldn't be said of Louis D'Ascoyne Mazzini, the coolly calculating murderer played by Dennis Price in the dark Ealing comedy, Kind Hearts and Coronets. One by one, Mazzini kills off all ten of the people who stand between him and the title of the Duke of Chalfont. Eight of these hapless victims are played by Alec Guinness who was equally adept at playing baddies such as the

James Mason's saturnine good looks

Herbert Lom was a convincing baddie

creepy pickpocket Fagin in David Lean's production of Oliver Twist. An inspired performance that, despite Guinness's preposterous false nose, prompted actor John Hurt to nominate it the film that changed his life.

The other villain in Oliver Twist is that thoroughly nasty denizen of London's underworld, Bill Sikes, played with chilling gusto by Robert Newton. Sikes is even cruel to his faithful dog, Bull's Eye, and no tears are shed when he is eventually hanged for the murder of his girlfriend, Nancy. Newton brought the same gusto to his most enduringly famous role, Long John Silver in Treasure Island. Born in Dorset, he used his West Country accent to great effect – Aharr, Jim lad! He went on to play the title part in Blackbeard, the Pirate. Newton is happily celebrated (and endlessly imitated) every September on national Talk Like a Pirate Day of which he is naturally the patron saint.

In real life, a pacifist who loved cats and country music, on screen James Mason was most often cast as a handsome but sinister character. His dubious reputation was established early on in a series of melodramas made by the Gainsborough studio that included Fanny by Gaslight, The Seventh Veil and The Wicked Lady. Margaret Lockwood played the wicked lady of the title, a beautiful aristocrat who decides to impersonate the notorious highwayman Captain Jerry Jackson (James Mason). When he discovers what she has been up to, they join forces and embark on a tempestuous but doomed affair.

In a distinguished career, Mason's saturnine good looks and mesmerising voice ensured him a succession of chilling roles including that of smoothly ruthless Phillip Vandamm in Hitchcock's North by Northwest and the role that few other actors would have been brave enough to tackle, tormented paedophile Humbert Humbert in Lolita.

Poetry Corner
The Saga of Mary Ellen's Teeth
By Verona Coppack

On Thursday we went to the theatre
We went on a mini-bus coach,
Not one of us there under 70
But not one of us there liked to fuss

We headed off there very nicely
No problems at all to start off,
Then poor Mary Ellen, who's 80
Suddenly started to cough

She spluttered and coughed something awful
Then as quickly stopped with relief
Till she shouted with such a loud voice to us all,
'Oh heck! Oh where are my teeth?'

We established they hadn't been swallowed
So set out to look on the floor.
We all crawled around looking foolish
Till all of our knees were quite sore.

Mary Ellen just couldn't forget things
She sat and continued to moan
'What will I do? I can't even chew
When we stop for our chips on way home!'

We finally got to the theatre
We had really good seats near the stage
A show full of mystery and magic
A show that would suit any age

We really enjoyed the first half of the show
And old Mary Ellen was fine
Different magicians were doing their tricks
We all had a really good time.

Then at least, nearly over, the top of the bill
The best of the best – plain to see
He waggled his wand and said funny words
We didn't know what we would see!

Full of anticipation and all goggle-eyed
We stared in amazed disbelief -
Because there, in the spotlight, in front of us all
We could see Mary Ellen's lost teeth!

Now I've no idea how he did it
It's something that we'll never know
But I can't help being very suspicious
Of our grinning coach driver – Joe!

So on the way home we all stopped for our chips
And Mary Ellen was able to chew
We'd had such a good time in spite of it all
And agreed it had been 'a good do!'

'Why do you talk

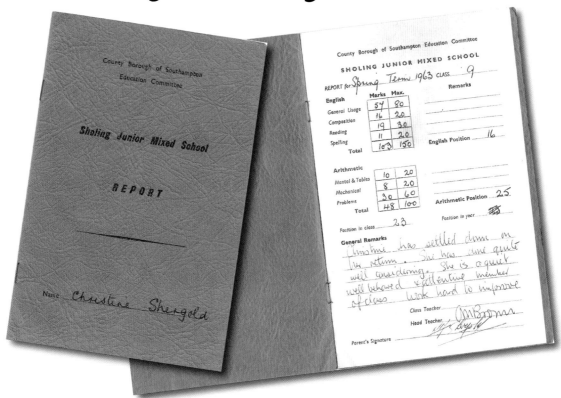

County Borough of Southampton
Education Committee

Sholing Junior Mixed School

REPORT

Name Christine Shergold

County Borough of Southampton Education Committee

SHOLING JUNIOR MIXED SCHOOL

REPORT for Spring Term 1963 CLASS 9

English	Marks	Max.	Remarks
General Usage	54	80	
Composition	16	20	
Reading	19	30	
Spelling	11	20	
Total	103	150	English Position 16

Arithmetic			
Mental & Tables	10	20	
Mechanical	8	20	
Problems	30	60	
Total	48	100	Arithmetic Position 25

Position in class 23   Position in year

General Remarks Christine has settled down on her return. She has done quite well considering. She is a quiet well behaved intelligent member of class. Work hard to improve.

Class Teacher

Head Teacher

Parent's Signature

Christine Baggs recalls her schooldays on the move as an army child

It was 1960, I was eight years old, and my army family were returning to England from another spell abroad. As usual, we went to Southampton to live with family and I returned to the local school, Sholing Primary, for a month or so while the arrangements for Dad's next posting were put in place. Mr Brown, the headmaster, took me to my new class where I had to stand in front of the other pupils while the teacher explained that I would be joining them for a few weeks only. At break, I was asked the usual questions: Why are you only staying for a few weeks? Why do you talk like that? My different accent always made children in the local schools laugh, but I didn't mind. As far as I was concerned, they were the odd ones.

When Dad's next posting came through it was to an army base in Tidworth, Wiltshire. We were allocated an army quarter and when we arrived all our boxes had been delivered and were piled up in the lounge. First Mum went through the inventory with someone from the Quarter Sergeant's office. Not until every knife, fork and spoon had been counted, furniture and beds checked for damage, then paint work inspected for marks would she sign the inventory.

During the time we lived in Tidworth I attended two different schools. The first was an army school and my arrival followed the usual routine whereby I was taken to stand in front of the class. However, this time I knew some of the other pupils, having been in the same class in Cyprus. It was all rather lovely, as it felt like rejoining the family. I was asked a question that never arose in civilian schools, and that was: "What rank is your father?" My answer established my place in the pecking order.

As you can imagine, in an army school with a constantly changing class, the teacher had a hard task finding work we could all do. However, the classes were small so there was time to work

like that?'

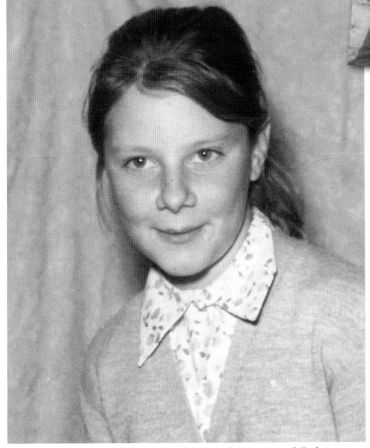

Christine's legacy from school is being able to walk into a room full of strangers

different to an army quarter. For a start, the walls were not distempered, but had wallpaper with picture patterns. In the lounge the pattern was houses, over all four walls. We children were allowed to number the houses, although it was impressed on us this was a one-off. We could only write on the walls because the paper was coming off very soon. It certainly kept us occupied one very wet weekend.

I went back to Sholing School and once again Mr Brown the Headmaster took me to meet my teacher. By now I had acquired a Wiltshire accent so once again I sounded funny to the other children. Used as I was to small classes, it was a shock to be placed in a class of 42, squeezed on to long benches so that the only way out was if everyone in front filed out first.

Because of my wasted term at the civilian school in Tidworth, I was now behind with work, but I had always done so well before that Mr Brown was confident I could catch up in time for the Eleven Plus. My school report for that term states, 'Christine has settled down on her return. She has done quite well, considering'. Mr Brown's faith in me was justified and I scraped through the Eleven Plus.

The legacy of my school experience is that I have never been afraid of walking into a room full of strangers. And I know how to build a periscope!

with each of us individually and I didn't fall behind. Unfortunately, it was decided that the Army Education Corps would be disbanded. The first to go were the army schools, so I had to transfer to the civilian school in Tidworth. The teacher in my class in the new school simply could not cope with the influx of new children, all at different stages of education. I remember him trying to add up the register, without success. I was bored and chatting and was warned that if I didn't keep quiet he would make me do the task. I never could keep quiet so the next thing I knew he

had me up on the podium and the register was put in front of me. I was told to add each column then add each row then make a grand total. At my first attempt it balanced! After that he gave up trying to teach us anything at all and instead we spent a whole term learning how to make a periscope.

About this time Dad had a choice to make. He could either accept a Commission or he could leave the army. He decided to leave and enter the civil service.

So we made our final move back to Southampton and Dad bought a house. It was so

A Christmas miracle

BY: KIM LEWIS

Ruth finds things don't always go according to plan

Her first term as a teacher at St Matthew's primary school was drawing to a close and Ruth Thomas was looking forward to spending the holiday with her family back home in Wales. But first she had to get the Year Six children word-perfect for the Christmas concert.

Three performances were planned; two in the school hall and one at Hollytrees care home to entertain the residents. A lot of time had been spent practising the carols with Ruth accompanying the children on the school's ancient piano.

She feared she had taken a bit of a risk in giving the solo of Once in Royal David's City to Melanie Stark. Melanie was a timid little girl but she blossomed when she sang, her voice amazingly strong and crystal clear.

At the end of their final rehearsal, Ruth told the excited children: "You did really well!" She was relishing her new life. Teaching was all she had ever wanted to do even though she had made some sacrifices to achieve her goal. One of them was the decision to move to England to get a job and another was parting with her boyfriend, Rhys. Their separation had been amicable but Ruth still missed him.

The first concerts performed for family and friends went well. Ruth felt proud that there had been no obvious mistakes or flat notes and both the children and their parents thoroughly enjoyed themselves. Some of the parents helped with the refreshments afterwards and there was a lovely friendly atmosphere.

The headmistress's praise: "Well done, Ruth!" meant a lot to her. Now all she had to do was to

Some of the parents helped with the refreshments afterwards

get the children through their last performance at Hollytrees. After that, it would be time to go home to family and friends. She felt in need of a rest and looked forward to her mother's legendary Christmas dinner.

On the day of the final concert, she woke to discover that snow had fallen during the night. Living in the north of the country, the children were used to winter weather so, dressed appropriately, they walked through the snowy streets to the care home. They were greeted by the manager who showed them into the large day room.

Once the children were assembled in front of the elderly residents, Ruth took her seat at the piano. She scanned the faces of the audience – some of them looked interested, some were clearly quite excited and some looked bored. She noticed a tiny lady in the front row who was sitting very still with her hands clasped in her lap and a smile of expectation on her face. Ruth hoped

ILLUSTRATION: KATE DAVIES

The girls on either side of her nudged her helpfully but Melanie remained frozen. Ruth replayed the opening chords. Suddenly a clear voice sang the opening lines. But it wasn't Melanie. All eyes turned to the petite lady in the front row. She sang the first verse faultlessly and the surprised pupils joined in the second verse.

At the end of the concert, Ruth thanked everyone for listening and gave a special mention to the unexpected soloist. Afterwards, while mince pies and hot drinks were being served, the manager said to Ruth: "I can't tell you how pleased I am. Honor came to us two months ago after her husband died. She's been very quiet and withdrawn – until today."

Ruth said: "It's amazing how music can be the key to our emotions," and happily reassured a sheepish Melanie that far from ruining the afternoon she had actually prompted a small miracle.

The last day of term arrived and the children tumbled out into the playground, thoughts of Christmas whirling round like snowflakes. Eager for home herself, Ruth was disappointed to find that her train had been cancelled. She would have to travel tomorrow instead. As she walked back to her flat she noticed a familiar car parked in the lane. Standing next to it was Rhys!

"Thought you might like a lift home," he said.

Ruth was taken aback by how thrilled she was to see him. "Whatever are you doing here?" she asked.

"I had something to do in York. It seemed silly not to stop off and see you."

"Doing what in York?"

He grinned. "Well, you always said I should go to uni. I've been accepted at York, starting in September. We will practically be neighbours."

Ruth laughed and hugged him. "Come on, you can drive us to Sainsbury's. We need dinner. There's no point setting off until the morning."

Outside the supermarket, the Salvation Army band was playing Once in Royal David's City and Ruth knew that memories of this Christmas would stay with her always.

The first two carols went well and some of the old folk joined in the singing

that all of them would be uplifted by the music.

The first two carols went well and some of the old folk joined in the singing. Next was Melanie's solo. As she took up her place at the front, Ruth noticed she looked more nervous than when she had been in the familiar surroundings of school. She played Melanie's cue, the introduction to Once in Royal David's City, nodding firmly at the girl whose mouth opened obediently, but no sound came forth.

We had stars in our eyes:
TRUE-BRIT HEROES

Kenneth More felt the role of Douglas Bader was his destiny

PICS: REX SHUTTERSTOCK

Many of the men who acted stiff-upper-lip heroes in war films had themselves served in the Second World War. They had first-hand experience of battle, knew how to salute correctly – and they all looked terrific in uniform!

Probably the best-loved of them all was John Mills who had the distinction of playing more military roles than any other star, 31 films in all. Several of these (In Which We Serve, We Dive at Dawn and The Way to the Stars) were, in fact, made during the war. He excelled at playing ordinary men who, when tested in battle, prove to be loyal and brave, but he could also put a different spin on the military type as he did in the role of emotionally torn Colonel Basil Barrow in Tunes of Glory (his own favourite film).

Jack Hawkins exposed the trauma of war in The Cruel Sea, a film praised for its realistic depiction of the hardships of service life and the difficult decisions that have to be made by leaders of men. As the captain of a corvette, Captain Ericson has to give the order to drop depth charges that he knows will kill his fellow countrymen as well as destroy the enemy. Hawkins was so moved when acting this appalling dilemma that the tears seen rolling down his face are genuine.

The Cruel Sea featured two other actors who were often cast as tough, tight-lipped types. Ericson's second-in-command is Donald Sinden, appearing in his first film, and rugged Welsh actor, Stanley Baker, as the bullying first officer.

The horrors of war were not glossed over in

Virginia McKenna trained hard for her role as an SOE

John Mills had more military roles than any other actor

Reach for the Sky in which Hawkins' lifelong friend, Kenneth More, brought every ounce of his acting talent to the role of Douglas Bader, the fighter pilot who loses both legs in a flying accident. Filmgoers were deeply moved by his personal battle to learn how to walk with artificial limbs and eventually to fly again, only to be shot down and taken prisoner by the Germans.

Richard Burton had been proposed for the role but More felt that he was destined to play it, saying: "Bader's philosophy was my philosophy. His whole attitude to life was mine."

Despite some controversy surrounding his own wartime record, Trevor Howard epitomised English stoicism in many of his officer roles. In The Cockleshell Heroes he plays Royal Marine veteran, Captain Hugh Thompson, who is initially scornful of an inexperienced officer's reckless idea for a night-time raid on the harbour of Bordeaux but consents to take part in the doomed exercise. As a result he is captured by the enemy and executed. Even in his most romantic role as Celia Johnson's rejected lover in Brief Encounter, Howard keeps his passion reined in. Famously a hellraiser in real life, he commented that he loved the iconic film 'but the role wasn't me at all'.

Courage in the face of danger wasn't the sole preserve of men. In Carve Her Name with Pride, Virginia McKenna played Violette Szabo who became a Special Operations Executive operating behind enemy lines. Not quite a true Brit (Violette's mother was French), she nevertheless fought bravely and gave her life for the allied cause. To make the film, McKenna had to be pretty tough herself, spending weeks learning unarmed combat, jumping from a parachute training platform and wading through an ice-cold lake at night.

Poetry Corner
Precious Memories
By Hazel Mills

It's strange the things I can recall
From the days when I was very small
First day at school, I remember so well
Polished floors with a lavender smell.

Summer days that lasted forever
May to September, just beautiful weather.
A British holiday at a West country beach
Golden sand for our play, that stretched beyond reach.

My big sister's wedding and my bright yellow dress
And eating too much, which made such a mess.
Hallowe'en that was scary, but not held in the street
Would be years before kids would go trick or treat.

I remember Guy Fawkes' night, the family fun
The big baked potatoes provided by Mum
A bonfire and fireworks that lit up the street
My brother and sisters with me at their feet.

Then Christmas, oh, what joy that would be
A gift from our Uncle, a real Christmas tree!
Waiting for Santa, hoping and praying
That the dolly I longed for would come and be staying.

But I threw a tantrum and sulked with a frown,
When I saw she was missing from Woolworths in town
But come crack of dawn on Christmas day
There she was in my pillowcase, waiting to play

Those were the good days, now I sit and recall
I pray all my life, I'll remember it all

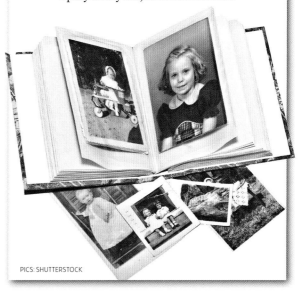

PICS: SHUTTERSTOCK

The magical mill

The back of the mill and the mill pond, showing the sluice

Sue Croxford's childhood playground was her grandparent's still active family grain mill

When I was growing up, I thought nothing of the fact that there was a massive water wheel at the end of the house, a mill pond in the back garden and a secret garden hidden from the outside world. My grandparents lived in an 18th century water mill that was used to produce animal feed. We would visit them every week and it is only now that I realise what an extraordinary place it was and how lucky I was to have known it.

My great-grandfather, George, was the manager of Longwick Mill in Buckinghamshire and eventually bought it in 1920, establishing GB Gomme & Son.

His son was my grandfather, Fred, and the business was later passed on to his children. My memories are of a time when Fred was semi-retired, living in the Mill House with my grandmother, Violet. Fred was tall and always wore dusty blue overalls, except for Sundays. My grandmother was round and cuddly and always wore a flowery dress with an apron tied around her waist.

The Mill House was a pretty white building, with blue window frames and a blue door. Stepping inside, the hallway had large flagstones on the floor that were worn and shaped by years

of footsteps. Each one seemed to be a slightly different size and colour and dipped in the middle. Whenever I walked up the hallway, I would take giant steps, making sure I only stepped once on each stone. At the end of the hallway, you reached the kitchen. It had a huge range with a kettle permanently warming on it. There were always lots of cats around the mill (I assume to keep the mice at bay) and they usually gave birth in a box by the warmth of the range. This meant there always seemed to be kittens to cuddle and play with.

A door led into the mill building and going through it

house

Left: My brother holding up the fish (and plastic bag) he'd caught in the mill pond. Above: My mother and grandparents, in their 'Sunday Best', in the garden of the mill house

was like stepping into another world. The mill was a mass of pulleys, chains, chutes and all sorts of contraptions that would give Health and Safety a fright these days! There were sheets of cobwebs hanging from the beams and everything had a thick layer of dust on it. Apparently my grandfather used to knock the cobwebs down every now and then, but they'd be back the next day, so he gave up trying. I can remember scurrying up wooden ladders, worn by years of use, which led up through hatches to the next floor. The very top floor had massive hoppers full of grain that we would jump into when nobody was looking and wade around in. From the outside, I remember my uncles waving to me as they stood in the doorway on the second floor. From there they would throw the filled sacks down on to a truck parked below, just as their father and grandfather had done before them.

The gardens were Nan's pride and joy. Every time we visited, she would take my mum on a tour, both with their hands clasped behind their backs. Always taking the same route, they would discuss the state of this and that and stop to smell whatever happened to be in flower at the time. I would trail along behind and amuse myself, snacking on whatever was ripe. The conclusion of the tour would be a walk past some sheds and garages. We would step through an archway and be in what I always thought was a secret garden. Completely hidden from view from the outside, it was full of large flowerbeds, bursting with all sorts of cottage flowers. Between the flowerbeds were neatly trimmed thin grass paths that made a trail to follow around the garden. I always believed it was a secret place that only a select few people knew about.

The wooden water wheel stopped being used when electricity was put into the mill, however it was still in place. I don't remember ever seeing it moving and some of the big blades were missing where it had fallen into a state of disrepair. It was fed by a mill pond that had a sluice gate to control the water flow. The pond was full of wildlife and was edged by marsh plants and enormous bull rushes that towered over me. My brother used to fish there, but without any success. One time my great-aunt felt so sorry for him that she bought a sardine and attached it (plastic bag and all) to the end of his line. He was so proud to actually catch a fish!

The front of the mill house, with the mill buildings to the right of it

Recipe index

Fish

Desserts

Cakes and bakes

Just for fun

Visit Pedigreebooks.com

to view our full range of titles.

Annuals

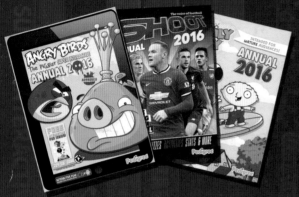

Fun Learning

Activity Annuals

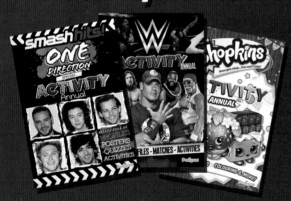

Yearbooks

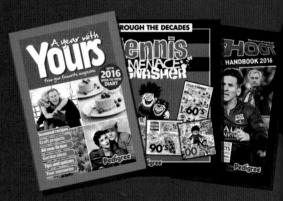

Pedigree®

THE #1 ANNUALS & YEARBOOK PUBLISHER

Pedigree Books, Beech Hill House, Walnut Gardens, Exeter EX4 4DH